Marianne Craig is a well-known health campaigner, researcher and teacher. She researched and wrote the first edition of this book while she was a member of the Women and Work Hazards Group.

Eileen Phillips is a writer, lecturer and researcher who has worked in the fields of equal opportunities, and women and new technology.

Marianne Craig
for the Work Hazards Group

New edition by Eileen Phillips

Office Workers' Survival Handbook

**A guide to fighting
health hazards in the office**

Illustrated by Angela Martin

The Women's Press Handbook Series

First published by BSSRS Publications 1981
Revised edition first published by The Women's Press 1991
A member of the Namara Group
34 Great Sutton Street, London EC1V 0DX

British Library Cataloguing in Publication Data
Craig, Marianne
   Officer workers' survival handbook. – New ed.
   1. Great Britain. Offices. Hazards
   I. Title II. Phillips, Eileen   III. Work Hazards Group
   363.1′19651

   ISBN 0–7043–4201–4

Phototypeset by Input Typesetting Ltd, London
Reproduced, printed and bound in Great Britain by
Cox & Wyman, Reading, Berks

Contents

Acknowledgments

We would like to thank Maggie Alexander of the London Hazards Centre for all her help, and for her considerable and careful work on the manuscript.

Grateful acknowledgment is made to the following for permission to reproduce copyright material:

The GMB (Britain's General Union), for the summary of the hazards of microwaves and checklists in *Hazards in the Health Service* (GMB, 1984).

London Hazards Centre for the sample questionnaire on RSI, in *Repetition Strain Injuries – Hidden Harm from Overuse* (London Hazards Centre Trust, January 1988).

NALGO for 'Draft questionnaire for identifying the causes of stress', in *Tackling Occupational Stress* (NALGO June 1988).

Trades Unionists Against Section 28 for material from *Out at Work: Campaigning for Lesbian and Gay Rights at Work* (Trades Unionists Against Section 28, PO Box 1733, London W9 3SH).

Every effort has been made to find copyright holders; we would appreciate being notified of any corrections or additions to the above list, and apologise for any omissions.

Foreword

I am pleased to introduce this new, improved version of the *Office Workers' Survival Handbook* updated by Eileen Phillips. Ten years have passed since I wrote the first edition. These ten years of Thatcherism in Britain have been hard, with savage attacks on civil liberties, trade unions and the welfare state. We have seen the widespread introduction of privatisation and the pervasion of an 'enterprise culture' and a commensurate lowering of health and safety standards. Unemployment has continued to be unacceptably high, while temporary, low-paid work is replacing permanent skilled work in many areas. 'New technology' is no longer new and has entered our homes and our workplaces on a scale undreamt of ten years ago.

Things were by no means rosy in the late seventies when I wrote this book, but there was a confidence and an idealism on the Left and in the Women's Movement which gave rise to an explosion of progressive ideas. These in turn continue to have an important impact on trade unions.

In 1975 I was involved with the British Society for Social Responsibility in Science. We were trying to develop a critique of science and technology (militarism, genetic engineering, environmental issues) and some of us came to concentrate our energies on occupational health. The growing interest in this field was partly fuelled by the introduction of the Health and Safety at Work Act in 1974, which gave workers more rights. People were beginning to extend an analysis of the pollution of the outside environment to the workplace, with health and safety conflicting with the pursuit of profit. We found that much research into occupationally-related diseases was hidden away in scientific journals. We wanted to communicate that information to working people, those exposed to chemical and other hazards. The trade unions and the health and safety inspectorate did not seem to be doing enough to protect workers. We set up Hazards Groups, publishing pamphlets and organising courses on health and safety at work. Along with other women, I soon became impatient with the fact that in the 'Hazards Movement', male-dominated jobs were presented as the most hazardous (construction work, mining), while 'women's jobs' (hospital cleaning, office work) were seen as clean and 'cushy' work. We formed the Women and Work Hazards Group in 1977 and published leaflets and organised conferences and courses for women on health and safety in the broadest sense. We included issues like childcare, sexual harassment and stress, as well as back pain, chemical hazards and VDUs. This had a profound impact on the growing health and safety movement, with its network of local groups working within trade unions all over the country.

It was during my involvement with the Women and Work Hazards Group that I discovered how little was written about the health hazards office workers face. I set out to write a pamphlet (a very old tradition on the Left – if you have something to say, write a pamphlet). I started to gather information, the files grew and the pamphlet became a book.

In Britain today, office work is characterised by low-paid, repetitive, badly designed jobs, mainly done by women, often black women, who are subordinate to white men in positions of power. Women *still* carry the burden of housework and childcare and still often do two jobs, consequently suffering very stressful lives. New technology has not helped them.

New technologies or information technologies permeate our lives. Office work has changed a great deal in these ten years but new technology is only part of the story. A radical restructuring of office work has taken place. New technology has been part of a whole set of organisational and political changes, with large-scale privatisation, cutbacks and efficiency savings. There has been a drive to a greater centralisation of control in the amassing and processing of information. There is much greater control of people too – careful monitoring of the workforce, for example, monitoring the number of keystrokes, or logging the numbers of clients processed. To some extent there has been a *re*-division of labour in offices, with women still occupying effectively the lowest-paid jobs – many as operators of the new technologies.

And what about health and safety? Many manufacturers now claim that their equipment is designed ergonomically. Yet there is no evidence for such claims. For example, there have been no surveys of ergonomically-designed chairs or desks. There are no standards, no requirements, no laws relating to the new technologies. The UK Government Health and Safety Executive, together with the employers' representatives, are currently opposing a proposed EC Directive to legislate for minimum VDU health and safety standards. The British Trades Union Congress is in favour of some guidelines on the matter. However, they would prefer a code of practice recommending broad guidelines and are opposed to specific regulations. This is disappointing since codes of practice are extremely weak and can be ignored by employers. Legislation is a starting-point that unions can build on.

In the last ten years office workers' lives have become more stressful. High-pressure management techniques, new technologies and fears over job security combine to make it so.

It is widely believed that the traditional approach to tackling stress at work is simply to negotiate better working conditions for members. However, I firmly believe that while such negotiations are crucial, we must acknowledge that stress grinds people down, makes them ill, feel powerless and demoralised, and often unable to participate in their union. This is especially true of women who have to juggle their many responsibilities and inevitably are made exhausted by them. Thus we need to look at ways of helping people improve the quality of their life, as well as ways of supporting them through their crises. This is in keeping with the true origins of trade unionism. Methods of coping with stress (relaxation, branch discussions about stress, information about counselling and alternative medicine, assertiveness training and stress at work courses) can be taken up by a trade union branch – thus they are taken up within a collective framework. This is very different from employers' initiatives on 'stress management' which should be treated with caution.

Trade unions were originally created for working people to support each other and to tackle problems collectively, including health problems. They were about building a community. There is a need to return to such fundamentals and this may mean finding completely new ways of working through problems like stress in today's offices.

I wrote the *Office Workers' Survival Handbook* to communicate information about health hazards to the office workers exposed to them. The book stood – and still stands – as a useful guide to the individual office worker who is isolated for any reason, to help her demand a better deal from her employer. If you can show your boss in print that staring at a VDU screen for hours can strain your eyes, this can help you negotiate better conditions. But I also raised issues of collective action and trades unionism: you have more power if you join with others in your attempt to win better conditions. As a feminist, I emphasised the exploitation of women in white-collar work and in the home.

Despite ten years of quite significant advances, the trade union structures are still largely male-dominated – even those unions with a majority female membership still have a majority of male officials and sexism is rife. The male shop steward as 'hero' rushing around doing everything *for* his members is still extremely common. This man may be very committed but he may also have an ulcer and does not necessarily know how to involve his members fully. It is women, by and large, who raise health and safety issues at work. It is women who are most concerned about their health. And one of the biggest changes that has occurred since I wrote this book is that the trade unions have now taken on board 'women's' and health and safety issues to some degree. Women in recent years have made a big push to be taken seriously. There have been many struggles, often unpublicised, about such issues in the workplace. Some of these struggles are documented in this new edition.

Today most unions with a large female membership have women's committees and in the last ten years these committees have fought for, and to a certain extent made, important gains. They have won some structural changes within the unions which have allowed them to meet separately from men and to *set their own agendas*. In this way they have run women-only courses, with topics chosen by themselves, producing materials such as women's health packs. Many unions now have health and safety departments or officers. Sometimes all this amounts to mere rhetoric spouting out of head office. However, it can be seen as a step forward. Thousands of safety representatives have been elected and they regularly inspect workplaces. Many have attended the TUC's 'Inspect and Protect' courses.

With a shrinking workforce, cutbacks and 'casualisation' of labour it is absolutely essential that such gains are not lost. Issues like racism, health and childcare, which are central to working people's lives in this country, were once marginalised by the unions, but a big push during the seventies and early eighties when unions' strength was growing put them in the mainstream. As times get harder the unions may be in danger of returning to such a marginalisation. And in an atmosphere of swingeing cutbacks in many sectors, there is a danger that these still central issues could be forgotten.

There is a pressing need for many more women to become truly active in their union. This is not easy given the restrictions on many women's lives. But if unions become more responsive and more flexible, and organise and *promote* women's courses including assertiveness training, they could grow again and truly represent working people everywhere.

It is now 1990 and environmental issues have exploded onto the political agenda. Thatcherism is on the defensive and 'green issues' are part of the counter-offensive, as is the increasing resistance of working people through their trade unions. Pollution and ill health in the workplace are an important part of environmental politics. The health and safety of working people is part of the same struggle as saving the rain forests or laying down standards for healthy food. There is a mounting popular awareness, and struggle to combat the social causes of ill health, which include poverty, bad housing and an unhealthy environment. These are not chance factors but reflect the distribution of wealth in society and the pursuit of profit – which until recently has largely taken precedence over the pursuit of health. There is a change in the air. There is a light at the end of the tunnel and I believe it's green.

My thanks to David Albury, Alan Dalton and Jenny Webber for our 'Ten years on' discussions.

Marianne Craig
London 1990

Introduction

Office jobs have become women's jobs. In these days of equal opportunities there is the occasional male secretary and the odd woman executive who is not simply supervising other women but taking her place in a man's world. But the general rule is that the person tapping into a VDU or answering the telephone is a woman. She may be extremely efficient and provide the backbone of the organisation, recognised or not, but she resembles a servant: a servant to the company, the public or to a particular man as boss. The fact remains that her role can be defined as helping the wheels to move, providing the mechanical means for accomplishing goals, meeting targets and achieving productivity.

Couple this with how women's relation to work, to having a job, is understood and one can see why there are massive problems in developing an acceptable set of conditions for working women, let alone improving the basic terms of the deal on offer. Women's contact with work is always seen as either temporary or about serving, facilitating and tidying up after the real business of making things happen has been done. This view of women means they will put up with anything – glad to have a job at all, or else unsuspecting that they are owed anything different.

Fortunately, the assumptions don't quite fit the reality. Women *have* questioned the deal and continue to do so. One of the most surprising ways they have done this is to change a tradition in which organised labour concentrates on rejecting the pay on offer, or fights for improvements in the wage packet. This shift has meant challenging what effects the 9 to 5 has on the health and sanity of those doing the time. Why should earning a living mean daily headaches, damaging your eyesight, pains in the stomach and a stress level that jeopardises the rest of your life? Why not demand from management that a job should not seriously damage your health just as much as it should allow you to pay the rent and bills?

Joanne Varley who works on a VDU in an office in Bradford from 8.30 to 4.45 wrote to City Centre, an office workers' resource centre in London: 'The staff have asked for breaks, but all the management say is: "When you feel tired or your eyes are sore, take a break of 5 or 10 minutes." If we do this, though, we are accused of working lazily.' Her experience is not an unusual one, particularly for those office workers without the protection of a trade union. Bosses are in the position of being able to demand relentless work that presents a serious hazard to your health. Despite the common belief that office work is clean, with plenty of tea-breaks and time to chat, the reality is usually much harsher. Modern office blocks with their sealed windows, artificial ventilation, fluorescent lighting, electronic equipment and synthetic furnishing materials are often the most damaging places to work – 'sick buildings' which can give staff constant headaches, colds, eye strain and backaches. New technology, while having the capacity to remove drudgery from typing and filing, often means that women are confined to a workstation in front of a screen, their work speeded up and routinised to fit with the 'needs' of the machine. As well as the stress on your eyes and mind that numbingly repetitive work involves, operators are exposed to low-level radiation, which may lead to all sorts of reproductive damages, whether she is pregnant or not.

Many of the health hazards in office work are hidden or denied by both management and the medical personnel they employ. The aim of this book is to uncover the increasingly well-documented health threats that *do* exist in most offices. It also shows the office workers who have fought back, winning significant concessions from managers and gaining a crucial sense of control over their working lives. You have a right to a safe and healthy job. As the World Health Organisation states: 'Health is a state of complete physical, mental and social well-being, and not merely the absence of disease and infirmity.'[1] Section 2 of the Health and Safety at Work Act 1974 states that it is your employer's duty to ensure your health, safety and welfare at work. You should be able to work in a job that does not grind you down with stress, that gives you access to canteen facilities, rest rooms and well-run nurseries, and where the deal being struck with your employer is not loaded against you.

This handbook should help you raise health issues at work and organise better to prevent hazards. Legal, practical and organisational routes exist which can take you out of a work situation that is wrecking your health. And they are routes that show the problem is not with the individual worker who is careless of her own health, but in the workplaces that force people to over-work using inadequate equipment, inhaling toxic fumes and biting their lips when their supervisor tells them to get a move on. Answering back as an isolated person can be a difficult as well as a risky business. But there are ways to make sure changing an intolerable set-up is done collectively so no one can be dismissed as a troublemaker or even dismissed at all. By raising health and safety rights with the people you work with, finding out how they feel, tracing particular hazards and agreeing a strategy, you will build up a confidence and capability in the whole office, or even throughout the company, which will encourage you to challenge management's prerogative to tell you what makes your job acceptable. After all, they're not the ones glued to a screen eight hours a day, answering telephones while printers thump out noise, photocopying for hours at a time or crammed into an overcrowded office.

One of the key issues facing office workers is the degree of stress they suffer at work. Life is fast these days – grabbing take-away food on your way to the cash dispenser at the bank, squeezing into packed buses and trains to try to get back in time to pick up your child from the child-minder and then catch the late-night shopping at the supermarket. If all this is on top of pressure forty hours a week, to do the work of three people, your mental and physical health will begin to break down. With cutbacks in local government and companies increasing profits by shrinking their workforces, and with unemployment at a level which makes the prospect of losing your job a threat, it is workers' health which is put at the bottom of any list of priorities. Reversing this dynamic may be a slow and painful process but it is a feasible one. Healthy and safe working conditions are unlikely to be handed out on a plate. But by putting the arguments persistently and backing them up with direct action, improvements *are* introduced. Office work has changed dramatically and workers have gained some important rights via trade union organisation and legislation which, although limited in its scope, does proscribe certain significant health dangers. There is a framework for staff to pursue health and safety, to monitor working practices and to insist on their employers taking responsibility for the health and welfare of their workforce.

Taking stock of the changes that have occurred both in the nature of office jobs and in the power of office workers to improve the working conditions offered them is an important means of realising that we do not have to put up with what we've got at the moment. The biggest change, which has had all sorts of significance for how work is organised in the office, has been the influx of women into office work. In the 1870s the typewriter was introduced and women were considered best suited to using these machines. Incorporating women into what had until then been an exclusively male environment was an innovation. In 1874, the Post Office established a grade of 'lady typist'; however she had to resign if she married. There were very clear stereotypes about which jobs were suitable for men and for women. The men who worked in offices were 'gentlemen clerks', who could still aspire to promotion.

However, by the early twentieth century, office work had become a problematic job for men. David Lockwood, in *The Blackcoated Worker*, describes the ambiguities which were expressed in popular fiction at the time: ' "Don't we lose our manhood?" ' asks the blackcoated hero of an early twentieth-century novel as he reflects on his job. ' "What do we see of real life? What do we know of the world? We're a small breed. We aren't real men. We don't do men's work. Pen-drivers – miserable little pen-drivers – fellows in black coats, with inky fingers and shiny seats on their trousers – that's what we are." '[2] It was more important than ever for men to distinguish them-selves from the women who were entering office jobs in ever-increasing numbers – if they weren't 'manly' compared to men doing physical jobs, at least they could have a higher status than the women who worked in their firms, and who were restricted to the most routine jobs, with no potential for moving up the hierarchy. As *The Business Girl's Handbook* made clear in its sobering advice to women looking for office jobs, there was a definite place for them, but it was not one they could expect to move out of:

For the quiet girl who is not averse to routine work there is a certain fascination about work in a bank. The bank clerk has a certain social standing which is very delightful. And her work, while quite well-paid, is not particularly exacting when once learned. It is more easy for you to enter a bank than it was for your brother, for many of the male appointments are made by nomination. . . . You may be surprised, on arrival at the bank, at the almost childish simplicity of the work set you to do. . . . But you must persevere with these simple tasks just as your brothers did in their first year at the bank.[3]

The 'brothers' having done their apprenticeships could expect to move on to more interesting and demanding work, whereas women could only expect to move at all by marrying and being forced to leave. This very rigid sexual division of labour set the scene for today's offices where, although men and women may work in the same office, nine times out of ten women will be doing the lower-grade work or servicing the men in their jobs.

Secretarial work is perhaps the clearest example of women's subordination to men. The 'office wife' may be asked to collect his clothes from the dry cleaners, order flowers for his wife's birthday, buy his sandwiches and, in times of crisis, soothe his furrowed brow and fend off unwelcome callers. Many women resist these demands, insisting that they are employed to administrate, organise, type and take notes for the organisation, not for the man himself.

Yet in 1990 it is still possible for a woman to be sacked for not co-operating with this hidden agenda. Carol, having worked for a number of years as an extremely efficient secretary, got a job in a small recruitment agency which had promised to offer her training to become a recruitment officer. She was pleased to have got what she had been led to believe was a promotion, a job with prospects. However, two weeks into the job, she found one of the male executives continually asking her to make him coffee and fetch him sandwiches. Eventually, she pointed out, mildly, that it wasn't really part of her job and that she was supposed to be being trained to do a job similar to his own. That night she received a phone call telling her that they had decided she wasn't really 'suitable' for the kind of work they did at the agency, and she needn't bother to come in the next day. As she put it: 'It really set me back. I'd been so pleased to get what I thought was a great opportunity, doing something that was going to stretch me. And then I suddenly found I was back in the same old situation where you're at the beck and call of some man, and he wasn't even my boss. I feel shattered now, my confidence is really gone, like I've been slapped down for stepping out of line.'

Alongside the entry of women into office work, the way work

was organised began to change in the 1920s. Just as in manufacturing (the assembly-line), work in the office has been analysed and divided up into minute, simple tasks. 'Scientific management' has meant that jobs are specialised, removing the control over how a job is done and at what speed, by preventing individual workers from having a grasp over the whole process. Understanding and decision-making become concentrated in the hands of managers who supervise groups of workers doing the different tasks which make up the overall flow of information-handling and administration.

The full logic of creating a 'clerical factory' has only approached its goal with the introduction of computers and word processors. An account by Barbara Garson of working in a data-processing centre at a clearing bank tells graphically of the stress and total lack of control that these new jobs involve.

> Tuesday, 10 a.m. Once again I'm led into a windowless room. Once again my job is to transcribe little bits of data from little slips of paper. . . . Although my eyes and neck ache a little, I don't really mind my second day. At six o'clock I punch out. But Florine and the two other black operators don't budge. . . . Unlike us temps, the staff workers have no regular hours. They have to stay until all the day's transactions are entered. . . . Leaving early for a sick child might mean $100,000 in interest lost overnight.

By the beginning of the next week she is getting unbearable neckache.

> Monday morning. I've rested all weekend, but after five minutes my neckache is back. Stress, they'd say and prescribe exercise or analysis (depending on my income). . . . So I go to the supervisor. 'Kurt, I don't like to tell you this, but something came up at lunch. I'm going to have to . . .' He sighs. It happens a lot. 'Nobody white ever stays,' a woman whispers as I punch out.[4]

A woman writing about her work in England again emphasises the dehumanised aspect of many clerical jobs:

> People who perform passionless routines among hostile machines [are] squashed flat by office pyramids and pecking

orders. . . . Most people don't seem to see that *office life* is a contradiction in terms. Office walls act as filters or transformers, dulling and dehumanising every aspect of human existence. . . . Our offices gobble up our best hours and real energy, drained of which we return (at six, seven, eight) to the homes and relationships which are supposed to be the most important things in our lives.[5]

Jobs have been constructed in this way in the interests of profit and to squeeze maximum productivity out of a workforce which is expected to sacrifice its health to earning a wage. But work does not have to be like this; office workers can demand to be treated like human beings rather than an extension of the machines they operate. The choices that have been made about work organisation, about managing clerks and typists, about dead-end jobs, are all ones that can be made again. Different ways of running an office, of taking decisions, of dividing up jobs, could be found, so that staff not only are not damaged by work but may even look forward to going into the office.

Trade Unionism

Looking back to the earliest efforts to organise against unscrupulous or indifferent employers, old problems have changed but not completely disappeared. Many nineteenth-century clerks were reluctant to join trade unions. They identified them as organisations for the labouring classes. The gentleman clerk relied on the goodwill of his employer and often worked in socially isolated situations. The earliest attempts to start unions were in the large offices – the civil service, railways, banking and insurance. At the beginning of the twentieth century the National Union of Clerks established a 'Clerks' Charter':

The Clerks' Charter

1 A wage that will enable them to live as educated citizens
2 Healthy and comfortable offices wherein they can work and keep sound mind in healthy bodies
3 Hours that will not leave those minds and bodies exhausted at the end of the day, but will leave them leisure to develop their faculties and their individuality.[6]

Both the Association of Women Clerks and Secretaries and the National Union of Clerks campaigned for inspection and improvement of office conditions and for better pay. They worked closely together and finally merged into the Clerical and Administrative Workers' Union, known as APEX, which in turn has merged with the GMB (General, Municipal and Boiler-makers' Union; now Britain's General Union). Other white-collar unions were formed later and have been growing ever since.[7]

Clerks in the nineteenth century had a high mortality rate, with expectation of life only 75 per cent of the average (plumbers 81 per cent, miners 85 per cent). The main killer was tuberculosis and other respiratory diseases caused by badly ventilated, damp and insanitary offices and crowded travel to and from work.

In 1911 the National Union of Clerks (NUC) began a campaign to fight tuberculosis and to have offices protected by legislation similar to the Factories Acts. Their Clerks' Charter stated:

> Clerks who do not help to get the NUC Inspection Bill through Parliament are by their *Apathy Helping in the Manslaughter* of thousands of their fellows. The death rate of clerks from lung disease is *twice* that of the ordinary population.

In 1916 in the United States women clerks could expect the shortest lives of all occupations – again due to tuberculosis. As late as 1930, the International Labour Organisation recorded 'consumption' (tuberculosis) as a major occupational disease for office workers.

> When you see a pale-faced multitude of clerks, victims of tubercular and nervous trouble, you may be sure that the impure air and unhealthy conditions of offices play a large part in the holocaust.[8]

In a job that involved a great deal of copying, 'writer's cramp' was common, and the clerks' unions succeeded in having it recognised as an industrial disease. But pneumonia, heart disease, fatigue and digestive disorders were also occupational diseases of office workers, and the last three still are. In the newly mechanised offices of the early twentieth century, workers were exposed to the jangling of telephones, the clatter of typewriters and to the danger of gas explosions. Eye strain and nervous disorders continued to plague office workers. And until employers were legally required to improve working conditions under the Offices, Shops and Railway Premises Act (OSPRA) 1963, dirty, overcrowded rooms lacking ventilation and natural light, and with insanitary toilet facilities, were common.

The campaign to include offices in protective legislation was won after fifty years of union activity. OSPRA provided a basic minimum standard. In 1974, after more trade union pressure, all workplaces were included under the Health and Safety at Work Act. There is little documentation about the struggles of office workers and their successes in negotiating better conditions, but many have done so and many continue to. Some of their stories are told in this book.

Bernard Shaw once said that the two groups most resistant to trade unionism were clerks and women.[9] Times have changed. In the last ten years female membership of trade unions has increased by 60 per cent, partly owing to the growing numbers of women workers, but also because of the greater activity of white-collar trade unions at least half of whose membership is female. Trade union membership in offices has more than doubled since the late sixties. However, offices in the private sector, which have small, disparate workplaces, remain poorly organised. Office workers' history is like that of farmworkers – traditionally isolated and exploited. The problem isn't as bad in the public sector or in offices that are part of the manufacturing sector. There may be divisions between blue-and white-collar workers within factories, but both groups are firmly embedded within a tradition of trade union organisation. Office staff in small legal businesses, accountancy firms or insurance companies face an uphill struggle in winning union recognition from their employers.

Some workplaces have 'house unions' or staff associations which never threaten industrial action and are prepared to be co-opted by management rather than negotiate on behalf of their members. They may offer fringe benefits and lower subscription rates than TUC-affiliated unions. It is only when the 'privileges' that management insist exist are revealed as hollow, unable to protect the members from redundancy or from having their hours of work increased or to ensure that promotion is not a matter of managerial whim, that staff association members begin to think of joining an independent trade union.

When it comes to health and safety issues, there is an over-whelming argument for the advantages of unionisation. It gives you the right, under the Health and Safety at Work Act, to elect a safety representative who can then claim rights to infor-mation and inspections. And, of course, it is when people start seeing that a union can be a vehicle for improving their working lives by preventing dangerous machinery being used or getting a new ventilation system installed that they develop a commit-ment to the union they may have rather half-heartedly joined.

Women and Trade Unions

Trade unions have finally woken up to the fact that women comprise more than 40 per cent of the workforce. As union membership declines due to the shrinking of sectors of the economy where unions have historically been strongest, new recruitment strategies for gaining female membership are being pursued. Attempts are being made to grapple with the problems of organising temporary and part-time workers. Both the Trans-port and General Workers Union (TGWU) and the General and Municipal Boilermakers (GMB) started to revamp their images in 1987 and recruit the part-time, temporary women workers who are becoming a growing proportion of the work-force.[10]

Whether these initiatives are able genuinely to tackle the need for flexible, shorter working hours for men and women alike or whether they expect simply to knock the new recruits into shape as 'regular trade unionists' remains an open question. Despite the fact that the proportion of female members in the major white-collar union ranges from 20 per cent (in MSF) to as high as 69 per cent (in CPSA),[11] there remains a reluctance to under-stand how women are forced to juggle badly-paid jobs with inadequate childcare provision. It also remains the case that officials and most union representatives are, by and large, male. Not because women members are incompetent or indifferent to union matters, but rather because they continue to be denied the chance – or rarely encouraged – to use their skills actively to negotiate on behalf of their fellow workers.

A male APEX rep, who was dealing with redundancies in the manufacturing sector, was astonished when he was accused of sex discrimination after he had admitted writing to all the women on maternity leave asking them if they really did want their jobs

back. As far as he could see, many women didn't come back, so why push a man out of his job when the woman didn't really want it? The fact that the difficulties of combining waged work and childcare can deter women from returning, or at least might make them susceptible to pressure from management, let alone their union reps, shouldn't mean accepting these 'facts of life'. Protecting women's right to work can only be effective when it also means campaigning for improved childcare arrangements, maternity rights, parental leave, and so on.

Within trade unions women's groups have been formed at both branch and national level. MSF, NATFHE, NUPE, NUT and NALGO all have groups which are successfully attracting women into active trade unionism. Just as this handbook shows that eradicating health hazards has to start from the experience of the workers facing them, the strength of these groups lies in their providing a space for women to say what is important to them, what their priorities are for changes at work. Everybody needs information if they're going to argue with managers, but nobody needs a sermon. Telling workers what is good for them is something that management specialises in. It shouldn't be what workers' own organisations reproduce. This handbook aims to help people find out what they need to know to take on the argument with their bosses, but equally importantly suggest ways of making sure that office workers themselves are heard.

Notes

1 World Health Organisation. First Principle of the Constitution of the World Health Organisation, signed 22 July 1946.

2 David Lockwood, *The Blackcoated Worker* (London, 1958).

3 *The Business Girl's Handbook* (London, 1926).

4 Barbara Garson, 'Scanning the office of the future', in *Mother Jones*, July 1981.

5 Janet Watts, *The Observer*, 29 October 1978.

6 *Clerks' Charter*, published by National Union of Clerks (NUC) in 1910. For more information about struggles in offices for better conditions in this period, see *By Hand and Brain: A History of the National Union of Clerks*, published by NUC in 1957.

7 During the sixties and seventies white-collar trade union membership increased dramatically: between 1964 and 1974 it went up by 58 per cent, see G. S. Bain and R. Price, *The Growth of White Collar Trade Unionism* (University of Warwick, 1976). The Banking, Insurance and Finance Union (BIFU) membership rose from 56,300 in 1964 to 116,730 in 1978.

8 National Federation of Professional Workers, *A Much Needed Measure* (1926).

9 Will Thorne (leader of GMBU in 1914) made this comment: 'women do not make good trade unionists and for this reason we believe that our energies are better used towards the organization of male workers' (in L. S. E. Webb, Trade Union Documents, A. XLVII, f.111; cited in Standish Meacham, *A Life Apart*, Thames & Hudson, 1977, p. 106).

10 Changes in the numbers of women working and the types of office work they were entering are shown in the statistics for the previous decade, along with a massive increase in part-time jobs for women:

June 1975–85	Men %	Full-time % women	Part-time % women
Banking and bill discounting	+17.2	+22.2	+64.0
Medical and other health services	−9.5	+0.07	+32.7

11 Female membership in the white-collar unions

Union	Total Membership	Female Membership	%
MSF	653,000	126,000	20
UCW	197,616	49,404	25
NUCPS	118,394	42,686	36
NALGO	754,701	391,216	52
BIFU	168,404	91.719	55
CPSA	143,062	98,262	69

Figures taken from: Trades Union Congress, *Congress Guide*, September 1989, pp. 51–6.

1
Stress

Do you get headaches and have 'bad nerves'? Do you often get indigestion or stomach aches? Do you sometimes feel irritable or depressed? Do you find it hard to relax in your time off because you're stiff and tense? The pressures on you at work and at home are probably the cause. Everyone's body reacts differently to pressure and every woman has her breaking point. Some stress is normal to life, but if stress is repeated or prolonged the body becomes exhausted and illnesses can result: ulcers, high blood pressure, heart diseases, nervous breakdown.

Because people experience symptoms of stress in mind and body it makes it easy for them to think: 'It's my own fault, I'm over-doing it', or 'I wish I was the sort of person who could relax more.' But it is important to remember that the causes of stress are not wholly the responsibility of the individual. Stress created by the job you do may be due to such things as bad work relations, violence and harassment, a gruelling shift system, monotonous tasks, being pushed too hard or being expected to accomplish the impossible with faulty equipment, a poor communications set-up and conflicting demands.

While the causes of stress should not be blamed on those suffering it, everybody can contribute to finding strategies for eradicating or preventing it. This chapter will discuss both the different reasons for stress at work and the best ways of tackling those pressures. There are solutions favoured by management and those pursued by trade unions, individual or collective 'coping' strategies, ones tackling the source of the problem or simply expecting to 'manage' it as an ongoing feature of working life. These different points of view need to be looked at carefully so that changes that really benefit workers in the long run can be achieved.

Stress is becoming much more commonly recognised as a cause of illness. Events in people's personal lives, such as the death of a partner, divorce, moving home or financial difficulties, are understood to have a direct effect on your physical and mental health. However, evidence shows that work is a *major* source of stress. In research undertaken at the Stress Research Unit, Nottingham University, in 1984, Dr Tom Cox discovered that over half of the 166 men and women he questioned doing both manual and non-manual work saw their stress as work-related, compared to one in five who saw it as home-related.[1] Similarly, a National Union of Public Employees (NUPE) survey of psychiatric nurses found seven out of ten gave work as the main cause of their stress compared to one in ten who said it was home-related.[2]

A conference held for trade unionists in 1988 showed many activists experience stress in their roles as negotiators and organisers. Strategies to lower stress levels were put firmly on the agenda of workers' organisations. For example, Jean Kitchen, a NUPE shop steward in a school, described the usefulness of relaxation methods: 'If I practise relaxation for a few minutes before I go in to negotiate with management I find that I win more for my members.'[3]

A recent victory for the trade union, MSF, in a damages claim pursued in April 1989 on behalf of one of its members in a computer services company, has shown that stress levels can be officially recognised: £25,000 was awarded against the company after a doctor testified that the stress being experienced by the worker was caused by conditions at the workplace.

Work-induced stress is often seen as concomitant with highly demanding, responsible jobs – executives cracking up in the face of boardroom pressures, senior managers collapsing with heart attacks brought on by work and worry overload. Yet the statistics relating to both causes of death grouped by occupation and absence from work for stress-related illnesses paint a very different picture.

The National Institute for Safety and Health (a US government department) has examined the health records of 22,000 workers in 130 occupations. They found the twelve most stressful jobs, in order of highest stress, to be:

1 labourer
2 secretary
3 inspector
4 clinical laboratory technician
5 office manager

6 foreman
7 manager/administrator
8 waitress/waiter
9 machine operator
10 farmer
11 mine operator
12 painter (not artist)[4]

Why do less skilled or lower-status jobs cause more illness and stress? A table compiled by Professor Cary Cooper[5] (of the University of Manchester Institute of Science and Technology) offers some answers.

Sources of Stress at Work

Intrinsic to job
Poor physical working
   conditions
Work overload
Time pressures
Responsibility for lives

Career development
Over-promotion
Under-promotion
Lack of job security
Thwarted ambition

Organisational structure and climate
Little or no participation in decision-making
Restrictions on behaviour
Office politics
Lack of effective consultation

Role in organisation
Role ambiguity/conflict
Image of occupational role
Boundary conflicts

Relationships at work
Poor relations with boss,
   subordinates or colleagues
Difficulties in delegating
   responsibility

Although some of these factors can be relevant to both high-status jobs and routine ones, most of them will be more familiar to workers in offices, factories or the service sector who have to face a lack of control over their time and decision-making while in their jobs.

Symptoms of stress can be both short- and long-term in their effects:

Short-term	Long-term
Headaches	Heart disease
Backache	High blood pressure
Tension/irritability	Stomach problems
Muscle cramps	Asthma
Poor sleep	Gynaecological problems
Indigestion	Depression
Period problems	Anxiety
Impotence	Peptic ulcers
Boredom/tiredness	Diabetes
Low self-esteem	Dermatitis
Accidents	
Skin rashes	
Eye problems	
Haemorrhoids	

Countless office staff work in huge bureaucracies, which have been described as 'honeycombs of depression'. The work you're doing can literally make you sick: work under pressure of time, to keep up with production quotas or deadlines, work that 'drives you crazy' because it's so boring – all these and more generate stress and anxiety. Office workers often keep tablets in their desks to get through the day, or take frequent time off.

When they go to their GP, the problem is treated in isolation, as a personal one. Connections are not drawn with work conditions or how co-workers feel. You're more likely to be given tranquillisers or have the early symptoms of stress – nervousness, headaches, irritability – dismissed as a 'female problem', the 'menopause' or 'your imagination'.[6]

Some workplaces employ company doctors who may suggest you're 'malingering' or have as their priority to get you back on the job as quickly and as productively as possible. Given that one of the symptoms of stress may be low self-esteem, employees may be particularly vulnerable to feeling guilty and inadequate, rather than pointing out that their department is under-staffed or their work too repetitive or that their boss is sexually harassing them. A review of work and stress at 35 large, UK-based companies, done in 1983 by the Stress Research and Control Centre at Birkbeck College, London, concluded: 'The findings indicate that only a minority of organisations are tackling the problem of stress directly. In these cases the orientation is directed merely towards the management of the problem, rather than prevention.'[7]

Locating the problem of stress in the workplace rather than a person's 'inability to cope' means taking a long, hard look at what's going on at work. This is obviously more threatening to management as it suggests they're not doing *their* job properly. However much they might want to reduce sickness and absenteeism and improve motivation, there is undoubtedly resistance to listening to what employees are saying about what's unsatisfactory in the way the company is run.

Causes of Stress

Physical Pressures

Bad lighting, poor ventilation, overcrowding and noise can all lead to stress. Bad catering facilities and crowded transport to and from work add to the problem. If you're having to sit at a VDU or stand all day filing you'll probably be aching by five o'clock. Repetitive movements and lack of physical exercise result in muscle fatigue – this in turn can be stressful. If you are anxious about your job, you are probably not sleeping well – another cause of mental fatigue. Physical and mental fatigue interact with each other to increase stress.

Pressures caused by work organisation and management practice

Anyone who has ever worked in a job which is a combination of tedious, boring, socially useless and over-regimented, and under close supervision, can attest to the stresses of work. If you find your job repetitive and boring, an insult to your intelligence, it's no accident. Management consultants are often employed to restructure office work. With the aim of squeezing higher levels of productivity out of employees, they may incidentally make the work more boring, increase the workload, and probably shed jobs along the way. As a result, most people are left working in jobs that are well below their potential. This 'rationalisation' is the result of 'scientific management'.

Early practitioners of scientific management applied to the office the basic concepts of the Taylor system, beginning with the breakup of the arrangement under which each clerk did his or her own work according to traditional methods, independent judgment, and light general supervision, usually on the part of the book-keeper. Work was henceforth to be carried on as prescribed by the office manager, and its methods and time durations were to be verified and controlled by management on the basis of its own studies of each job.[8]

All this means higher productivity from the worker while concentrating control over everything done at work in the hands of management. Keypunching is a good example. Your hands are occupied, your eyes fixed, you can't move your body, you can't talk. Many data-processing centres and typing pools are nothing more than clerical conveyor-belts, and the twentieth-century clerk has become a cog in a huge machine. The way office work is now organised means that mental labour has been reduced, the necessity for thought and creativity progressively eliminated. The jobs themselves have been carefully divided into numerous simple tasks, enabling the pace of work to be increased and eradicating any reliance on employees' skill.

Work overload is a direct cause of stress. A study in the United States looked at stress levels in twelve women invoice clerks who were put on piecework. They could attain a maximum of 400 invoices an hour, which gave a bonus of over 80 dollars for two days' work. Productivity was measured in terms of invoices per hour, with deductions for clerical errors. On piecework the output rose by 114 per cent. At the same time, the adrenalin in their urine rose by 40 per cent. (Adrenalin is secreted in the body when highly stressed.) Work has been measured to eliminate 'wasted time'. Speed-up increases production, efficiency and profits – and causes stress.

Machines can play an important part in speed-up. The technology which is supposed to 'make work easier' destroys jobs and leaves behind a faster work rate that forces employees to be paced by the machines. To call word processors, computer terminals (VDUs) 'user-friendly' is a euphemism for a system of simplified work which can be done more quickly and has less meaningful content. Speeded up, routinised work is work over which the worker has no control. Denial of decision-making, never being asked your opinion about how your office should be organised, close supervision either by machine or office superior, are all part of the experience of not being in control. The result is high stress levels.

Managers have greater control over their work. They are not confined to one place, they don't have to clock in and out, and they are not so constrained by 'superiors'. They have responsibilities and can participate in more decisions that affect themselves and others. All these, it is claimed, result in stress for the boss, but it is the *absence* of control and responsibility which is fundamentally at the root of the problem for many office workers. Interestingly enough, it has been pointed out that the assumed high level of heart attacks among top management is in fact intrinsic to the lives of *middle* management.[9] Facing both ways at once, they can feel the pressure to succeed in controlling subordinates while being subject to examination and control by higher management. A woman manager may feel she must 'prove her worth' as a woman entering a male-identified job. She can also encounter hostility from those she manages, colleagues and her bosses on the grounds of her sex. It's hardly surprising that these women are more prone to stress than their male counterparts.[10]

The Right to Rest

No rest-break is a real killer. Your job may be organised so that you have set lunch- and tea-breaks. But unfortunately, many office workers still don't have 'official' tea- or coffee-breaks. They make a cup of coffee or get one from a machine or trolley, then bring it back to their desk and carry on working.

An irony of a smoking ban at Camden Council, introduced in October 1988, is that some VDU operators are finally getting the breaks away from their screens that their union negotiated for them. As one put it: 'It's daft isn't it – the smoking ban is supposed to improve staff health – and what it's meaning for me is that I go to the smoking room for ten minutes every two hours. We're all supposed to stop keying in for that and we never did before. Now I get away from my screen to have a cigarette – good for my eyes, bad for my lungs!'[11]

Unless breaks are formalised, whether part of a new technology agreement or as a tea-break, it's highly likely that in a busy office employees won't take the breaks they need. Leaving your desk, telephone, VDU or typewriter just to stop work becomes an act of insubordination because, after all, your time at work is not your own, it belongs to your employer.

Flexitime may appear one way of making your time your own. Outside 'core hours', you can choose whether to come in early, work late and guarantee that you're not being pushed into working more hours than you should. For women who regularly have to juggle the demands of work and domestic tasks, it can seem a solution to the many impossible demands of the 'double shift'. But it also means you're clocking in and out; however much you gain from being able to 'flex' time off, you are under pressure to worry about minutes, you may skimp on your lunch-break when you need more rest, and you may be encouraged by management to be in the office only at the busiest times:

There used to be a much more relaxed atmosphere in the office. Some days you'd be busy, but others there was time to chat and take your time with a job. Now it's rush, rush, rush. When there's a lot to do the supervisor will make everyone stay late . . . and when it's a quiet day she'll say, 'Right, girls, why don't you leave a bit early today – take some time off.' When they're there, they're always under pressure.[12]

Working long hours without breaks makes you tired, more likely to have accidents and more stressed. Jobs with mandatory overtime are bad for your health as well as having the effect of helping keep basic rates of pay low and the number of available jobs fewer. And more and more office workers are on shift work, whether they are receptionists, switchboard operators or computer staff who keep computer centres running 24 hours a day.

Shiftwork damages your health and your social life. It disturbs your body's normal patterns for eating, sleeping and relaxing and upsets your physical and mental balance. If your employer is trying to introduce shiftwork it's worth organising a meeting of all those who will be affected to discuss the health side-effects. It might be worth preparing a leaflet to explain some of the health hazards and stressful effects of 'unsocial hours'.[13] You should also consider whether it will reduce the number of jobs and make it impossible for some people to work (some shifts are very difficult to cover for childcare). If bonuses are being offered, then what are you exchanging? Extra money won't be much use if you've neither the time nor the ability to enjoy it. If you are in a union you need to think about how shiftwork could affect union organisation.

Fitting women for work

Demographic changes mean that over the next decade there will be far fewer school-leavers available to take up the low-paid, bottom-of-the-ladder jobs – the ones often staffed by women. Banks and shops, among others, are in the business of finding ways of getting women back to work after having children. Job sharing, workplace nurseries, holding jobs open for up to five years, bonus payments for returners – these are just some of the incentives being used. Companies such as TSB, Boots, NatWest and the Co-op, in the face of persistent government refusal to provide any childcare facilities or increased employment rights, are finding their own ways of encouraging women to carry the dual responsibilities of a job and running a home.

While we can welcome the growing recognition that services must be provided if women are to take on the burden of the 'double shift', the fact that it is individual employers that are taking these initiatives opens the way to drawbacks for workers. As the limited local authority childcare provision shrinks because of decreasing resources, those women who rely on facilities provided by their employers have no choice about where or when they work. Women who are not in jobs that face labour shortages have to find makeshift solutions, and these often break down. They may then face pressure from their bosses: 'If you can't guarantee you can get to work perhaps you'd better stay at home with the kids.' This choice is rarely open to women in low-income families or single parents and so women toil on, making sure they go to work however ill they feel just in case they need time off for a child's illness. No woman should have this 'choice' forced on her: we have the right both not to be isolated in the home and to have access to financial independence.

Men too should have the right to work fewer hours and spend more time with their children. The limited concessions on reducing the working week gained during 1985–6 were less frequently won in the following year.[14] It remains easier to negotiate a wage rise or productivity deal than it is to achieve a shorter working week, even though the demand regularly appears as part of annual wage negotiations. Even when a shorter working week is gained it can simply mean more overtime working, despite trade union attempts to decrease reliance on overtime. With men working long hours and women forced into part-time work in order to cope with childcare responsibilities, the likelihood of equal responsibility for housework is minimal. And for women who want or have to work full-time, it is often the case that their partners expect the home to run as smoothly as before without increasing their own contribution to shopping, cleaning and arranging to collect and drop off children.

Violence at Work

Just as the different positions men and women occupy in family life contribute to the stresses of waged work, the forms of violence and harassment experienced by employees at work stem from life outside the workplace as well as power relations within it. As the government continues its strategy of dismantling the welfare state, diminishing local authority housing provision, squeezing income support for the unemployed, shrinking social services, the pressures and frustrations experienced by people using those services increase. These 'clients' may well vent their anger on the staff who are unable to give them any hope of the home or benefit they so desperately need. An entry in the incident book at Lewisham's Housing Advisory Centre in 1987 illustrates this dynamic: 'Refused to leave HAC after interview, demanding rehousing. Police called at 5 p.m. He continued to be abusive to them and was arrested.'[15]

It is possible for workers to win concessions over safety issues raised by tense and violent work situations. NALGO members in Brent staged an eighteen-week strike during 1988–9 to protest against the attacks they were suffering when attempting to provide a housing needs service. Screens were put in place to protect the staff from such things as jars of urine being thrown at them. A joint management and trade union working party was also set up to examine office layout and design and the possibility of special training.[16]

Although employers have a duty under section 2 of the Health and Safety at Work Act to take 'reasonably practicable' precautions to protect staff, it has been trade union pressure that has forced the Health and Safety Executive (HSE) to produce guidelines for employers about handling violence at work.[17] A number of unions have briefing packs which outline the steps that should be taken to prevent and respond to physical and verbal abuse of staff.

There are certain key issues involved:

- Can the risk of violence be eliminated by ensuring adequate staffing levels which prevent long queues and rising tempers?
- Are staff trained to spot violent situations developing?
- Can home visits be made in pairs and avoided after dark?
- Are personal alarm systems available?
- Are the offices used by the public designed to provide the maximum of comfort possible to those waiting and visibility for the staff?
- Are all incidents reported in a systematic way?

Conflicts may exist between the need to reduce stress and danger for the staff providing the service and the wish to be open and receptive to the public. An individual employee may walk the tightrope between 'giving their all' and so refusing to take precautions which they consider alienating to the client, and then encountering abuse or assault when they discover they are left vulnerable in an explosive situation. This dilemma may be a trade union issue such as at the Housing Advisory Centre in Lewisham, referred to earlier. Here NALGO members also went on strike to force management to install fixed protective screens. Management were refusing because they believed the screens would create an unnecessary barrier between the staff and people in need of housing advice. The London Hazards Centre was called in to investigate and discovered that there were a number of improvements that could be made to the layout of the centre, security provision and staffing levels.

Violence at work is not only a matter of relations between staff and public. It takes place within offices in the form of sexual and racial harassment, as well as discrimination against lesbians and gays. Although the HSE fails to include this in its report on violence to staff, during the last five years workers have succeeded in gaining widespread recognition that these types of harassment are both prevalent and a serious occupational hazard.

Sexual harassment can be defined as repeated, unreciprocated and unwelcome comments, looks, actions, suggestions or physical contact which is experienced as offensive and creates an intimidating working environment. Here are some examples of the situations and incidents that occur regularly in almost all offices and add up to a staggering level of sexual harassment suffered by women workers.

A colleague put his arms round my waist and pressed his body to me while I was holding the coffee tray.

When I was alone in the office with a man from another department he made a dive at my breasts.

I was in the office alone with my boss and he thought he would take advantage of the position – he half-raped me.

Jokes are the worst because they are not as obvious as someone pinching your backside, but just as humiliating. You have to respond in a particular way or you are a social outcast. But if you do laugh, you end up hating yourself. By laughing at a joke you don't find funny you are kind of accepting whatever idea the joke is based on.

When I was approached by a hospital porter in my first job I was young and naive and automatically assumed that I had encouraged him in some way. Ashamed and embarrassed, I left the job several weeks early.

Women are most likely to be sexually harassed by men who have power and authority over them at work. Couple this with the kind of scepticism which a woman can meet with if she complains to colleagues ('Can't you take a joke?', 'Come on, you're flattered really', 'Men will be men') and it becomes clear how difficult it can be for her to challenge this behaviour. It's easier to leave the job rather than go through the humiliations involved in proving your case against the harasser.

However, in 1986 a woman who complained of sexual harassment by two male colleagues, forcing her ultimately to transfer to other work, had her case upheld by the Edinburgh Court of Session. The judges ruled that sexual harassment of this kind was 'a form of unfavourable treatment to which a man would not be vulnerable' and was a weapon used 'against the victim because she was a woman'. This case firmly establishes that sexual harassment can be seen as sex discrimination under the Sex Discrimination Act 1975.[18]

Even when you're in a trade union and the union has a positive and sympathetic policy towards women who are being sexually harassed, it can still be a nightmare. An example in a West London factory shows this up starkly. A woman on the shop floor was being abused by her line manager who was in a position to control both her access to overtime and bonuses. It had reached a point where he was threatening to keep her wages down unless she agreed to his sexual advances. She took the case up with her union, the AEU. As Roger Butler, her district organiser, put it:

She's had a really rough time of it and it's not helped by a number of union reps inside the factory refusing to take it seriously. I've been doing my best to pursue the case for her but I'm finding I can never get hold of her to talk through the best strategy. She's off sick all the time and my guess is she's just going to leave because she can't stand the pressure she's under from this bloke.[19]

Racial harassment is another serious cause of stress in the workplace and again is linked to the fact that black workers are often forced to accept low-status jobs which allow those supervising them to abuse them. The harassment can be intentional or unintentional. It may in some cases involve physical assault but more often it's name-calling, excluding people socially or giving them orders in a rude and officious way. Feeling isolated in the office and knowing that if you complain you'll be called over-sensitive or labelled as having a chip on your shoulder means that many black workers put up with racist situations which raise their stress levels.

A black woman NALGO member was originally employed by Southwark Council as Clerical 1 Grade in its Legal Division. She applied for several posts as a legal executive within different sections of the Legal Division. She was consistently unsuccessful in getting higher grade posts. The Black Trade Unionist Solidarity Movement applied to an Industrial Tribunal on the grounds of racial discrimination, but the case was resolved internally and the woman was finally given the higher grade legal executive post.[20]

There are examples of sexual and racial harassment and discrimination against lesbians and gays being successfully fought through industrial tribunals and workers being compensated or reinstated. These are usually the most extreme cases and have required persistence and determination from both the worker concerned and the union or agency supporting them. The everyday examples which many workers cope with need to be prevented as well. These are often far harder to deal with, not least because the sufferers find it difficult to convince others that the harassment is real and damaging. For those who've never been on the receiving end, it can often be impossible to imagine how degraded and humiliated women or black people are made to feel by what's defended as 'just having a laugh'. Meeting as a group of women or black workers to discuss any problems that are being experienced can be a useful first step to resolving them. It is always harder to tackle an abuser by yourself. By attempting to win the support of colleagues or your union you can discover that you're not the only one suffering this type of harassment.

Lesbians and gays have no specific legislation to protect them against harassment and discrimination at work, although other laws may apply to their particular situation. *Out at Work*, published by Trades Unionists Against Section 28, holds the view that it is better to try to resolve the situation with the support of your union without resorting to legal action against employers, giving the following reasons:

- Courts and tribunals are biased towards employers and traditionally unsympathetic to lesbians and gay men.
- The laws on discrimination are inadequate and apply only to race and sex. The burden of proof is on the person complaining of discrimination, while any evidence of discrimination is usually held by the employer.
- Legal remedies are individual, not collective, so while individual victories should give more protection to all, employers are at liberty to ignore these judgements until challenged in court by another aggrieved individual.[21]

Misinformation about AIDS has increased discrimination and harassment against gays and lesbians in the workplace. Although lesbians are considered a low-risk group they may well suffer discrimination because of the level of misinformation and ignorance about the disease. A few cases have been won against employers refusing to give jobs to gay men. Dan Air lost a case against the Equal Opportunities Commission, on the grounds of sex discrimination, for refusing to employ male stewards (assuming that they would be gay, and were therefore an AIDS risk).[22]

What can be Done about Stress?

There are two different strategies in the face of stress: one is to cure it and the other to prevent it. Everyone can benefit from exercise, physical relaxation, healthy food and, in the event of personal or work crises, the use of a counselling service. However, as this chapter has shown, if the causes of stress are intrinsic to the work situation then remedies must be found there rather than in the individual's ability to cope.

Stress is largely a matter of feeling a lack of control. Clerical workers are often worn down over the years by their jobs and their employers, and feel that nothing will ever change, that nothing can be done. Discovering that this isn't true and that the situation can be back under your control is an important step towards alleviating stress. It may be a small victory that you win, such as the right to an official tea-break or improvements to the staff canteen, but it will have happened because you as office workers have made it happen. Success will encourage you to find out more about the health hazards and stress levels experienced in your office, perhaps by conducting a survey. Several unions have published model stress questionnaires for their members to use. A recent NALGO publication contains a useful questionnaire which can be used to help identify causes of occupational stress.[23] The more organised you are as a group, the greater chance you have of persuading management to listen and respond to your demands.

We also need stronger laws. Several states in the USA have awarded compensation to workers suffering from occupationally related stress, and section 12 of Norway's Work Environment Act should serve as a model for Britain. It contains several important requirements:

> Employees shall be afforded opportunities for personal development and the maintenance and development of their skills. Monotonous, repetitive, and machine or assembly work that does not permit alternation of pace shall be avoided. Jobs shall be designed to allow some possibility for variation, for contact with other workers . . . and production requirements and performance.

Stress is mitigated where there is greater job satisfaction. Work could be very different: instead of day-to-day tedium and meaningless tasks, work could be satisfying and stimulating. But this isn't going to happen until people start refusing to do the jobs that are draining them and ruining their mental and physical health.

Checklist [24]

Tackling occupational stress is an important but complex job and it must be done in a systematic way. This briefing has sought to provide information on relevant issues and to show the links between the individual causes of occupational stress. The following list provides both a summary and a reminder of the issues which need to be tackled.

Physical Environment

1 High standards of health and safety achieved, maintained and monitored
2 A human environment rather than a production process

3 Layout which is relevant to the type of work undertaken, such as telephone usage, level of concentration needed, dealing with the public
4 Spacious, well lit, well ventilated
5 Offers thermal comfort
6 Noise levels controlled

Equipment

1 Suitable for the job, user and the environment
2 Planned, frequent maintenance
3 Desks, chairs and other furniture ergonomically correct

Job Content

1 Provide opportunity for learning
2 Lead to some future desired by the job holders
3 Enable people to contribute to decisions affecting their jobs and the goals of the organisation
4 Ensure that the goals and other people's expectations are clear
5 Provide a degree of challenge
6 Provide training and information adequate to perform at acceptable levels
7 Individual tasks which:
a Combine to form a coherent job, either alone or with related jobs whose performance makes a significant and visible contribution
b Provide a variety of pace, method, location and skill
c Provide feedback on performance in a number of dimensions both directly and through others
d Provide a degree of discretion in carrying out successive tasks
e Carry responsibility for outcomes and particularly control of work

Management Style and Structure

1 Acknowledgement of the value of the human contribution to the organisation
2 Clear, well-communicated objectives
3 Consistent approach
4 Flexible enough to allow individuals a degree of control in their jobs

5 A proper balance between responsibilities and authority to carry out those responsibilities

Recruitment and Selection Procedures

1 Matching the job requirements with the skills, knowledge and experience of the applicants
2 Embodying a positive action approach

Training Arrangements

1 To plug any gaps in the skills, knowledge and experience of the individual and those required in order to do the job well
2 To extend the skills and knowledge of the individuals
3 To meet changes made in tasks, equipment and work practices
4 To deal with specific aspects of the job, such as the risk of violence at work, changes in legislation

The Management of Change

1 Discussion of the implications with trade unions
2 Information made freely available to unions and employees
3 The use of training
4 Allowing time to adjust

Hours of Work

1 Existence of shift working, unsocial hours
2 Flexibility
3 Rest breaks

Recognition and Other Service Conditions Matters

1 Payments systems and wage levels which are seen to be fair and reflect the contributions of individuals to the organisation
2 Holidays – the amount, the pay levels and the choice of when they can be taken
3 Procedures for dealing with grievances, complaints, discipline and dismissals which are seen to be fair

Support Systems

1 Nursery facilities
2 Transport for those working unsocial hours
3 Special provisions to meet special needs, such as maternity, bereavement and special leave
4 Flexible working hours and jobs to meet some people's temporary needs
5 Advice and support for stressed people
6 Confidential counselling

Notes

1 T. Cox and T. Brockley, 'The experience and effects of stress in teachers', *British Educational Research Journal*, Vol. 10, 1984, pp. 83–97.
2 B. Norfolk and J. Stirton, *Stress at Work – Preliminary Report* (NUPE High Royds Hospital, undated).
3 *Stress and Trade Unionists Conference Report 1988*, available from Doug Miller, TU Studies Section, Faculty of Social Sciences, Newcastle upon Tyne Polytechnic, Ellison Place, Newcastle upon Tyne NE1 8ST.
4 *National Safety News*, USA, January 1979.
5 Cary and Rachel Cooper, and Lynn Eaker, *Living with Stress* (London, 1988).
6 In its survey on VDU work and stress, City Centre reported that 50 per cent of respondents used pills and other drugs to help them cope with symptoms caused by poorly designed environments, and 78 per cent had taken sick leave in the last year as a result of these symptoms. City Centre, 'VDU work and stress survey', *Safer Office Bulletin*, March 1989.
7 See V. Orlans and Pat Shipley, 'A survey of stress management and prevention facilities in a sample of United Kingdom organisations' (London, 1983).
8 Harry Braverman, *Labour and Monopoly Capital* (New York and London, 1974), p. 307.
9 M. Lucas, K. Wilson and E. Hart, *How to Survive the 9–5* (London, 1986).
10 Bobby Jacobson, in *The Lady Killers: Why Smoking is a Feminist Issue* (London, 1981), points out that 42 per cent of women executives smoke regularly as against 30 per cent of men in similar jobs.
11 Personal communication with author.

12 A temporary secretary quoted in Jean Tepperman's *Not Servants, Not Machines: Office Workers Speak Out* (Boston, 1976).
13 See Labour Research Department, *Shiftwork and Unsocial Hours* (LRD Publications, 1987).
14 *Bargaining Report*, May 1987.
15 *The Daily Hazard*, No. 12, April 1987.
16 *NALGO News*, 3 February 1989.
17 Gail Foot, CPSA staff rep, DHSS unemployment benefits office.
18 Reported in *Labour Research,* April 1986, p. 21.
19 Personal communication with author.
    A useful model questionnaire designed to assess the extent of sexual harassment that occurs in workplaces is available from the Labour Research Department: *Survey on Sexual Harassment at Work* (LRD Publications, 1987).
20 'Racism, black workers and trade unions', *Black Trade Unionist*, No. 2, 1984, p. 7.
21 Trades Unionists Against Clause 28, *Out at Work: Campaigning for Lesbian and Gay Rights* (London, 1989), p. 7.
22 Ibid., p. 32.
23 NALGO, 'Draft questionnaire for identifying the causes of stress', *Tackling Occupational Stress*, June 1988, p. 16.
24 NALGO, 'Action checklist', *Tackling Occupational Stress*, June 1988, p. 17.

2
Office Environment

Noise can damage your hearing and cause stress. Most people associate uncomfortable noise levels with factories but an office with ventilation whirring, the heating system vibrating, the fluorescent lighting humming, typewriters clattering and phones ringing can be as great an assault on your nerves and ears.

Exposure to noise over a long period may result in the destruction of nerve cells in the inner ear, with a resultant loss of hearing which is both permanent and incurable.

Any hearing loss caused by noise will be added on to whatever you are going to suffer anyway as you get older. Even a small loss now will make you hard of hearing much sooner. Hearing damage doesn't just make sounds softer, it cuts them out and it distorts them. This can make life a misery, with you thinking people are muttering while they claim you're not listening. Deafness is isolating and ruins your home life as well as your health.[1]

A serious complication of noise-induced hearing loss may be tinnitus – a ringing, buzzing or thumping in the ears. This may be loud enough to cause permanent irritation and even prevent sleep.

Noise

Excessive noise affects your communication, sense of touch, clarity of vision, balance and coordination. It contributes to fatigue, loss of sleep, headaches and irritability. It can also cause rising blood pressure and an increased heart rate. Even if the noise level is low, it can be stressful if it interferes with your ability to communicate and concentrate. Studies have shown that office workers exposed to intense or even moderate noise have an increased incidence of circulatory, digestive, neurological and psychiatric problems.[2] An investigation of university staff with sedentary occupations found that after three days of systematic exposure to typewriter and aircraft noise, they complained of fatigue and irritability. The authors suggest the effect of the noise was a 'mild type of anxiety-depression syndrome'.[3]

A recent Finnish study of the outcome of pregnancy in women workers exposed to noise levels of 80 decibels (dB) or more found that when combined with shiftwork, the risk of threatened abortion was *double* that of unexposed women. The risk of high blood pressure in pregnancy was also doubled for women exposed to noise in shiftwork. Exposure to noise levels of 80 dB and over alone was found to increase the risk of growth retardation in the foetus. The greater the noise levels the women

Source	Decibel level
Leaves rustling	10–30
'Recommended comfort level' for boardroom	30–35
Director's office	20–54
Copying machine	62–68
Electric typewriter	63–69
Accounting office; average traffic at 100 feet; large shop; some electric fans	70 (West German 'acceptable level')
Hearing damage begins here	
Vacuum cleaner	74
Heavy traffic; office with tabulating machines; some electric typewriter carriage returns	80 (Dutch 'acceptable level')
Data-processing centre; single multilith printer in small room	86
Most factories; addressing machine	90
Electric staple gun; inside underground train/tube	(UK 'acceptable level')
Food mixer at 2 feet; unmuffled motorbike	100

were exposed to, the greater were the risk factors for all these effects.[4]

The following table shows how noise levels from office machinery compare with other sources of noise and the 'acceptable' levels recommended in different European countries.

An EC Directive obliged the UK to pass Noise Regulations by 1990. In October 1989 the Health and Safety Commission (HSC) published the *Noise at Work Regulations 1989* which came into force on 1 January 1990. Regulation 6 states that employers have a general duty to reduce the risk of damage to the hearing of their employees to the lowest levels reasonably practicable. The regulations introduce a new 'action level' of 85dBA. Noise is usually measured in 'A-weighted decibels' or dBA, which gives a reading with a filter switched in, thus mimicking the sensitive reception of the human ear over different frequencies and recording a better measure of the damaging effect of noise on hearing. The HSC admits that at this level 11 per cent of workers exposed for a lifetime will suffer hearing loss. However, only at 90dBA will stricter control measures come into force. At the 85dBA level employers have to:

- have a noise assessment made by a competent person
- keep records of assessment
- reduce risk of hearing damage as far as is reasonably practicable
- provide information, instruction and training to workers on the risks they face
- provide ear protectors to all who ask for them and maintain and repair them
- ensure that other noise control equipment is used and maintained

At 90dBA the employer is required, in addition, to reduce noise exposure by reasonably practicable means other than ear protectors.[5]

Audio typists are at particular risk at work. They risk a double dose of noise because cheap earphones may have to be played so loudly that, combined with the noise of surrounding machines, the ear may be receiving up to 90 dBs. Telephone operators' ears have been measured as receiving 87 dBs, enough to cause hearing loss. The International Labour Office's *Encyclopaedia of Occupational Health and Safety*[6] shows that when making long-distance connections there can be 'an intense audio-discharge' which is greater than the ear's capacity of resistance. This can lead slowly to deafness or acute laryngitis.

Measuring the Noise

Noise is measured on a logarithmic scale of decibels, based on powers of ten. This means that ten more decibels denotes that the sound is ten times as intense. It may not *sound* ten times as loud but it damages your hearing ten times as fast.[7]

Any sound source of 70 dBs or more may cause temporary loss of hearing, which in time may lead to permanent deafness. The average level in offices is 50–75 dBs and this level makes normal conversation difficult. The quality of noise is most important as a source of stress – irritation because of whines or hums, being startled because of sudden noise, the effort of trying to concentrate. The decibel level may not be very high, but you should trust your own response. If you want a decibel level to negotiate around, go for what's thought acceptable for executives' offices: 20–54 dBs.

Dealing with Noise

There are several ways of dealing with noise:

1 Reduce noise at source
2 Reduce it on the way to you
3 Reduce the time of exposure
4 Protect your ears.

Engineering controls to quieten machinery at source are the only acceptable answer in the long term. Management may say that it is impossible, but in the vast majority of cases it can be done. Often what they really mean is that the cost would be too high. The cost to whom? Not doing it could cost you your health. One typewriter manufacturer has reported that silencing materials on electric machines would only add 30 pence to manufacturing costs.[8] It's also worth pointing out to employers that they could face costly claims for damages from their employees. The GMB, for instance, won over £20 million in compensation for its deafened members during 1987.

In some computer rooms noise levels are above 85 dBs even after sound-proofing. Badly maintained equipment can be noisy;

regular maintenance helps reduce noise at source. Ideally, only quiet machinery should be installed in the workplace. Safety reps have the right to be consulted on new equipment. Office buildings, as well as office machinery, should be designed to be quiet. But architects are increasingly using cheap, lightweight materials which give rise to noise problems. Good floors and structures prevent noise in the first place.

In a badly designed office you may want some 'acoustic control'. Thick carpeting, acoustic tile ceilings, heavy fabrics and plants all help absorb some sound. To be effective, materials have to be light or 'fluffy' to stop noise being reflected. Baffles cutting off glare from fluorescent lighting should be made of sound-absorbing material.

Typewriters and teleprinters can be enclosed by 'hush boxes' to reduce sound. In one workplace, felt was used on RCA print-out equipment to lower the noise from 80 to 50 dBs. Mats under typewriters and other equipment reduce vibration and stop the desk being used as a sound box. Sometimes equipment can simply be moved. Buzzers or lights instead of bells on the phones, and rubber-tipped chair legs are other ways of cutting down irritating noises.

Outside traffic is one of the main noise hazards in offices. The GLC recognised this problem and recommended that traffic noise levels in 'executive offices' should not be above 45 dBs. However, they found it acceptable if levels in 'general offices' rose to 55 dBs.

A survey in France found that 50 per cent of all buildings are inadequately insulated. Builders should seal gaps round doors and air ducts. The Building Research Establishment has also published information on good quality double-glazing.[9]

At a General Electric plant in Ohio, in a large office area adjacent to the factory, advertising and product information employees were distracted by noise from the factory and complained about the 75–78 dB noise level in their offices. As a result the ceiling was re-suspended, the doors sound-proofed and the walls acoustically treated. Although these were important gains, this approach increased the separation of factory and white-collar workers. A joint union strategy might have succeeded in getting the noise reduced at source.

More space and less overcrowding may further reduce noise. Take a look at your boss's facilities – more than likely they're spacious and *quiet*.

If you're working in a noisy office, an interim measure could be more breaks. This doesn't solve the problem but is a feasible short-term demand. You could also try getting noisy equipment moved to another room.

A common management solution to noise in factories is ear-muffs and ear plugs. This is a classic cover-up operation which leaves the hazard untouched.

If you have to walk through a noisy factory or site, you should be provided with ear protection (this is also true for protection from dust or fumes) – though earmuffs and masks can never be a substitute for getting rid of the hazard at source.

Getting Something Done

Ask if anyone is suffering from ringing in the ears, headaches and other symptoms of stress, giddiness, difficulty in hearing others speak, especially when there are several talking, such as at a party. Do you have to raise your voice to talk above noise at work?

Record complaints in the accident book. This is useful to back up your case if compensation is being fought for.

You can measure noise levels by conducting a management noise survey, or one carried out by a health and safety inspector, or a consultant. If your employer won't agree, or if you don't trust the results, check with your local trade union health and safety group or a helpful local organisation. A survey done by the London Hazards Centre of shops in Oxford Street during 1986 showed extreme levels of noise, largely caused by loud music, up to 98 dBs.[10] You may be able to borrow a noise meter from a health and safety group and do it yourself. Section 6 (2) of the Regulations for Safety Representatives and Safety Committees refers to the reps' right to equipment necessary for inspection purposes. Try to use this section to back up your request to use such equipment. The survey should be done during normal working hours and not at 'quiet times' such as lunch-breaks. You also should be careful that the hearing tests are not used by management against workers to engineer transfers or redundancies. It's also important to remember that damaging and stressful noise is not only caused by high decibel levels. So if workers are complaining about stressful noise, changing the office environment should be tackled whatever the decibel level measured.

Lighting

Eye strain is one of the traditional health hazards of office work. Continuous reading of small print or scrawled documents in poor light puts an unnecessary burden on office workers' eyes. Not only can this cause headaches and eye inflammation, giddiness or double vision, it can lead to permanent damage to eyesight.

Section 8 of the Offices, Shops and Railway Premises Act requires that lighting in offices should be 'sufficient and suitable'. Although this is a vague standard, it can be used to your advantage and there are cases of complaints to the Health and Safety Executive leading to better lighting being installed in offices. Growing recognition of the dangers of flickering lights, glare, uneven or insufficient light has led the HSE to produce guidance on identifying and eliminating lighting problems.[11] This sets out clear methods for assessing how adequate the lighting is in your office and the different types of lighting arrangements available.

Artificial Light

By far the most disturbing aspect of the [Lloyds Bank Computer Centre] building is the relentless electric lighting. Only 15 per cent of the exterior is glazed, letting in very little natural light. 'The windows are only there for psychological reasons,' said West [the architect]. 'They don't provide any working light. You see, we wanted to be very energy-conscious.'[12]

Working all day in artificial light isn't good for you. In France there is a collective agreement for travel and tourist agency workers, incorporated into law, which gives an extra eight days' paid holiday to workers permanently employed in basements or constantly working by artificial light. This can be seen as selling health for 'danger money', but at least it recognises the danger.

A report produced by the Medical Research Council, Applied Psychology Unit, Cambridge, in 1988, showed that fluorescent lighting strips are a major cause of illness among office workers. The group investigated two groups of workers – one working under normal fluorescent lighting and one under tubes with virtually no flicker. Although this difference is not one that can be consciously perceived, it was discovered that the group working under flickering fluorescent tubes consistently reported more headaches and eyestrain.[13]

Such problems as glare, which either causes discomfort, dazzles or reflects distorted images, are dealt with in *Fluorescent Lighting: A Health Hazard Overhead*.[14] It also details the hazards of PCB's, the chemicals that store the electric charge in fluorescent lights. Although their use was banned in June 1986, any workplace with lighting that is more than two or three years old should investigate the light fittings and discard any PCB ones. This useful guide sets out ways of tackling lighting problems, using the law, your trade union and other action for pressuring management to implement improvements.

Natural Light

Such vapid and flat daylight as filtered through the ground glass window and skylights, leaving a black sediment on the panes, showed the books and papers, with the figures bending over them, enveloped in a studious gloom and as much abstracted in appearance from the world without as if they were assembled at the bottom of the sea. (Charles Dickens, *Dombey and Son*)

Daylight views allow restful 'visual pauses' during work. Windowless offices are hazardous. According to the International Labour Office, they cause an increase in disease and weaken the body's resistance to illness. Ideally, there should be plenty of daylight. The windows should be clean to let in as much light as possible. Your employer has a duty to keep them clean and free from obstruction.[15]

The 'sick building syndrome' is discussed in a later chapter but it is worth pointing out here that connections have been made between the ill health suffered by office workers which has been categorised as 'building sickness' and the absence of natural light. The Institute of Occupational Health in research covering six office blocks showed that headaches were minimised by maximising natural light and also returning the control of lighting to the individual worker.[16]

Some office workers complain of glare from sunlight. Blinds and low transmission glass can help. Double glazing with an outer leaf of solar-controlled glass and an inner leaf of clear glass will reduce glare and also control heat loss. Where large developments are built for speculative letting, architects often fail to attend to basic matters such as lighting. The occupying firms later partition the building into separate units, and many areas then have inadequate or uneven lighting. It is now possible to maximise the use of both artificial and daylight simultaneously by the use of photoelectric switches. When daylight falls below a certain level, the switches bring on the electric light. In addition, dimmer switches can be included which gradually increase the intensity of the electric light as the daylight fades. So there is no *technical* reason why you can't have good lighting in your office.

Action

If you are fighting for better lighting at work, aim for the best you can get. You will often find that what was put there by the architect is not what you want. One architects' journal is quite blatant about discrimination against office workers:

Some office and conference rooms may require status lighting, although discharge sources and particularly fluorescent tubes are the commonest sources for ordinary offices. Directors' suites and conference rooms often have quite different kinds of lighting, employing incandescent sources, either in ceiling mounted fittings or often, for directors' offices, in table lamps and wall brackets.[17]

But why should directors have expensive lighting when office workers don't? The need for good lighting is far greater for clerical workers, given the demands put on their eyesight by the work they do.

Conduct a survey of people's eyesight and try to find out if symptoms such as headaches are caused by bad working conditions for reading, writing and the operation of machinery. Demand a planned programme of cleaning and maintenance of all light fittings. If you think the lighting in your office is unsuitable, record complaints in the accident or incident book so that you can build up a case for improving or changing it.

Lighting is measured in units of lux, a measure of illumination on a particular surface. Different lighting authorities vary in the levels of lighting they recommend. The Illuminating Engineering Society (IES) has drawn up a code of lighting standards which is used as a general guideline in Britain. They recommend lighting levels of between 500 and 1000 lux for office work. 1000 lux is an inadequate level for reading small print, bad carbon copies, ink and pencilled notes: the IES code recommends 1500 lux for 'very fine work'.[18] But the American National Standards Institute recommends 1600 lux for most office work. Although fixed standards can be helpful, you should ask for what *you* find comfortable to work with. Older people need more light. The lux recommendations have been assessed for people under 40 years of age. Recommended standards must be increased by 50 per cent for those over 50 and by 100 per cent for those over 60.

Some typical light levels in lux

Very bright summer day	up to 100,000 lux
Overcast summer day	30,000–40,000 lux
'Bad light stops play'	1000 lux
Shady room in daylight	100 lux
Street lighting	20 lux

To find out how much light there is in your office, you can do a rough survey with a camera light meter (allow it to 'settle' in the light for five minutes). Or you can press management to do a survey. The health and safety inspector can do this too, while the local electricity board and the IES will offer advice.

Finally, a word about eye tests. If you think your eyes are being strained by your job, you can demand an eye test. But be careful that it is not used against you. No one should lose her or his job as a result of any kind of medical screening. Such screening is already widely used as a way of discriminating against the 'weak' who apply for jobs (older people for example). Make sure you get the results of any medical tests, but don't let them be a substitute for doing something about the problem. A process or product that ruins your eyesight is a health hazard.

Sitting, Standing and Strains

After a hard day at the office you probably have back pain or an aching neck and shoulders. This isn't 'just you'. It means your job has been badly designed so that you are having to sit or stand in a position for a long period, possibly repeating the same movements. Aches and pains also mean that your desk and chair are badly designed for your needs.

Normal muscular work requires alternate contraction and relaxation. This increases the rate of bloodflow, which easily removes the waste products the body naturally has but causes, if retained, fatigue. However, if a muscle is contracted for a long time without being relaxed or is held in one position, the muscle receives very little oxygenated blood and quickly tires. This is what happens when you repeat movements again and again, such as filing, writing, typing or standing or sitting for long periods in one position.

Traditionally, a clerk worked in a standing position at a high desk. Filing clerks still have to stand all day and varicose veins are one result. But since the late nineteenth century office work has become more or less a sedentary job entailing a stooping posture with the head forward and the back curved. If reading or writing are required the stomach may be compressed against the desk. This is bad for the lungs and impedes abdominal movement. Cystitis and constipation may be related to your job.

Badly designed chairs and prolonged sitting can also give you swollen feet or ankles. Constant sitting leads to slack muscles, especially if you stoop while sitting, say over a typewriter. A great number of office workers develop back strain caused by uncomfortable chairs and long hours of sitting with nowhere to rest the head.

In an Alfred Marks survey of office workers' health,[19] one in ten workers had *frequent* backache; 45 per cent said their chair did not support their back; 34 per cent found their chair uncomfortable. And according to the Back Pain Association, 56,000 workers in Britain are absent from work each day because of back pain.

Are You Sitting Comfortably?

In her excellent book *Women's Work, Women's Health: Some Myths and Realities*, Dr Jeanne Stellman outlines some of the problems of sedentary office work:

> A chair must allow a person to sit with a minimum amount of pressure on the thighs, which are soft and easily compressed; otherwise blood circulation can be blocked, resulting in pooling in the lower part of the body. This pooling causes the veins to dilate and can lead to, or aggravate, haemorrhoids, the very uncomfortable dilation and swelling of the veins at the opening of the anus. Blood pooling is also a complicating factor in varicose veins and other circulatory problems.[20]

Lisa Christie works as an office temp in Birmingham and says that many offices still have bad seating for typists:

> Often they look right and are theoretically adjustable but they won't move. Yet temps have to adjust to them all the time. Also some of the backrests are hopeless. You sit forward typing in a hurry and you don't notice you are off the backrest. In the place I'm in now – a plastics firm – the typist's chair is an ordinary dining room chair! My back's killing me right now.[21]

The Offices, Shops and Railway Premises Act states that seats for office workers must be suitable in design, construction and dimensions for the worker and the kind of work done. A footrest must be provided unless it is possible to support the feet

comfortably without one. Both the seat and the foot-rest must
be properly supported while in use.[22]

What exactly is a well designed chair? There are four key
factors:

The Height

A chair should be adjustable so that when you're seated your
hips and knees are at right angles and your feet are flat on the
floor. If you have to move your feet to operate a foot pedal
(e.g. on a dictaphone) an incorrect height can strain muscles in
your back and legs and even lead to muscle joint disease.

The Backrest

Many office chairs have adjustable heights but not adjustable
backrests. These are essential. A backrest (kidney-shaped ones
are best) should fit snugly in the small of the back so it supports
the spine and the lower back. It is not the back itself that is
primarily in need of support, it's the pelvis, so an adjustable
backrest should be positioned at the back of the waist. Your
chair is badly designed if you find you have to use a cushion to
support yourself.

The Seat

The chair seat should be slanted backwards just enough to allow
you to lean comfortably against the backrest, but not so slanted
that you slip too deeply into the chair and have to stretch and
strain to reach things. Some people prefer a seat that can also
tilt forwards because they find it more comfortable. The edge
of the seat should be 'scrolled' so it doesn't dig into the back of
your legs and the entire seat should swivel; that way, if your
work requires turning the torso your back will be supported by
the backrest as you turn. Many chairs with swivel seats become
unstable because of wear, so this must be taken into account
when you are choosing a chair. In some offices you only get a
swivel chair if you've got back trouble, even though it was
probably the bad seating that gave you the trouble in the first
place!

Sedentary work can deform your spine. Swedish research
shows the relation between posture and risk of damage to the

spine. Pressure inside the discs is considerably increased when the trunk is bent forward.[23]

Typists constantly have to turn their heads to one side to read what they are typing. This can cause twisting of the spinal column and shortening of the muscles on one side of the neck or back. An Italian survey of women operating calculating machines for many years revealed that they all had pains and muscular spasms, and their lower back movements were restricted, especially at the end of the working day. In each case X-rays revealed spinal deformities. The introduction of swivel seats, however, eliminated their pains.[24] A chair seat that is too long can also place undue pressure on the lower back and thighs, since it forces you to lean forward in order to work. A well-fitting seat will end approximately five inches from the crease behind your knee when you are sitting against the backrest.

Good seating can significantly improve serious back problems, as the Ergonomic Research Unit have shown. They give an example of a 45-year-old office worker who had had three bouts of sick leave due to acute low back pain. An examination of the office showed a mismatch between the desk height and the office chair. By improving both the work station and getting a more suitable chair her back pain disappeared.[25] A recent BSI draft standard, which was implemented in 1990, has this to say about chairs used for typing and VDU work: 'A well-designed chair should encourage a good posture that is easy to maintain, as well as providing unrestricted circulation in the thighs, minimising back strain and allowing a certain amount of movement while seated.'[26]

The Material

While some upholstery is desirable, it's important that the seat should be relatively hard. The pressure in soft or 'numbum' seats is invariably distributed widely over the soft tissues, leading to discomfort and anaesthesia of the skin of the buttocks and thighs. Chair seat material should be porous to allow normal body heat to dissipate. Cotton, textured fabrics are best (the texture prevents you from sliding forward); vinyl and other plastics do not allow body heat to escape. This is particularly important if you wear synthetic materials which trap body heat and increase perspiration and may be a cause of vaginal or bladder infections in women.

All office furniture should be well maintained and cleaned regularly. Armrests are important for comfort. But they get in the way if you're typing so a good typist's chair has none. The chair should be sturdy and firm. An unstable one may mean you have to keep back muscles permanently tense. Chairs on castors are not a good idea as the chair doesn't give support. It has to be held in position by tightening the leg muscles, causing muscles to become fatigued and sore. Castors are also potentially unsafe; one typist sustained a cracked vertebra when a chair fitted with castors slipped from under her. Perhaps the safest chair is a five-legged swivel chair; it is sturdy and can't topple.

Gas lift pedestal chairs allow for easy height adjustment but there have been reports of explosions in some makes where the control lever enters the cylinder through a round or keyhole-shaped aperture in the side wall. The Crown suppliers, who supply most government offices, recommended withdrawal of makes of chair with this defect after 27 reports of cylinder failure had been notified to the Health and Safety Executive in 1987.[27]

You can still find advertising brochures that offer chairs of very different quality and design according to the status of the employees – a simple wooden model for the typist, a more comfortable chair for the manager, while the most elaborate armchair is reserved for the president. And as one medical study concluded: 'If every manager were made to sit for a certain number of hours a day with his feet hanging, there would be an enormous increase in the number of footrests in our industrial plants tomorrow morning.'[28]

Desks and Tables

Many women are sitting at desks that are too high for comfort. A chair and desk should be considered together, as a unit, so it is not practical to give recommended heights for the furniture. (The British Standards Institution recommends 28 to 29 inches for desks for clerks, to be used with chairs of 17 inches. Such standards are always based on the 'average worker' – usually a man.)

Ideally the table, like the chair, should be adjustable to suit your particular health and comfort needs. The height you need will also depend on the kind of work performed, for example, a lower table is required for typing than for writing. It will also depend on the type of typewriter or electronic keyboard you are using. The height of the keyboard from the table varies considerably from typewriter to typewriter. Ideally the keyboard should be as low as possible while the cylinder (platen) should be at a level that makes it unnecessary for the typist to bend her head. One study in an Esso company office where workers complained of muscle and joint pains revealed that desks were too high.[29] You really want an adjustable typewriting/working desk combination where typing has to be done. It is also essential that desks allow for plenty of leg room, for legs need to be able to stretch out during work. There should be no obstructive middle drawer or moulding on the underside that can impede knee room.

It took many years of suffering by typists and key punchers before their complaints were taken seriously and ergonomists were called in to improve office furniture design. There is now a huge and growing literature on ergonomics (the design of machines and furniture). Much of it is unnecessarily mystifying and, as one contributor to an International Labour Office conference said in 1977: 'I have yet to find the textbook on design engineering which would concede so much as a chapter to the user, consumer, operator point of view.'[30]

Design of office furniture still leaves a lot to be desired. The best equipment is often prohibitively expensive. Needless to say, office furniture is *big* business and very profitable. But for all the glossy advertising and all the academic ergonomics papers, there is still no consensus on the ideal seat or desk. One German study concluded: 'there is no optimum seat shape that will suit all persons.'[31] A good chair or desk is what suits you, what *you* find comfortable.

But what if you're stuck with a chair that doesn't fit right or sit right? Stand up and speak out. Ask if you can have a better one. Find out if others are dissatisfied too. And ask your employer to obtain several types of well-designed chairs so that workers of varying builds can try them for comfort and suitability.

At the Leeds GPO the switchboard operators didn't like their newly designed seats and desks. As one woman put it, 'they didn't have any space for you to sit comfortably if you were pregnant . . . they must be a right load of idiots those designers'. What did the workers do? 'We sent them right back where they came from and told them to start again!'[32]

Many office jobs are badly designed. Over a third of the women in the Alfred Marks Bureau survey said they were *hampered* by the tools of their trade. Their chair gave no support and was uncomfortable, the stationery was out of reach, the filing was made difficult, and for one in four the telephone was out of reach. Good furniture design, good lighting and ventilation will go a long way to alleviating the aches and pains and muscular fatigue of office work. But they may not solve the problem altogether. In a French study of 590 typists, many had severe back trouble even when the best design of chairs and tables were introduced.[33]

The problem remains of women sitting in the same position all day, every day, doing the same repetitive job. If you are sitting for years doing the same task you will suffer. Good quality equipment, a job designed for satisfaction and health and plenty of rest breaks . . . when we have office jobs like that we'll see fewer aches and pains.

Repetitive Strain Injuries (RSI)

One of the most debilitating injuries suffered by office workers who have to sit at keyboards and type furiously and fast is RSI. In its guide to RSI, the London Hazards Centre defines RSI as follows:

> RSI is the term for a range of injuries to tendons, tendon sheaths, muscles, nerves and joints that result from doing repetitive movements or from overuse. Problems in the neck and back, shoulders, arms, elbows, wrists, hands and fingers are the most common, although other areas of the body can be affected.[34]

It can lead to permanent damage which disables a worker to the extent that she is incapable of picking up a cup or turning a key in a lock, as well as suffering severe pain. As one woman wrote in a letter to *Hazards Bulletin*:

> When a person loses a hand or a foot or is obviously crippled, there is at least some monetary compensation. When a typist gets RSI the onus is on her alone to prove she is ill. She may be going through days and nights of pain and agony (which most men would not be expected to put up with) but on top

of that she has to convince a panel of DSS doctors and lawyers that she is ill, because they cannot *see* the symptoms.

Then there is the financial hardship. I was out of work for eight months – for six months because I was in too much pain even to hold a pencil, let alone return to a typewriter, and the other two months because I couldn't find a new career that did not involve using my hands. Many women have even had to get divorces through having this disease because their husbands and families simply cannot understand how hard it is to do normal, everyday tasks and especially housework.[35]

Australia was the first country to recognise that RSI had reached epidemic proportions among office workers. There are at present around 50,000 keyboard operators employed by the Australian government who are attempting to sue their employer for work-related injuries. They have had to face denials and double standards from a government anxious to avoid compensating their workforce. On the one hand, the government established a National Occupational Health and Safety Commission to deal with the prevention and management of RSI (known as Worksafe Australia). On the other, RSI's existence was suddenly denied when fighting compensation claims. A Sydney rheumatologist, Professor Peter Brooks, claimed the severity of RSI symptoms depended on the sufferer's 'belief system'. Legal advice was given to the government:

> in conducting cases every attempt should be made to allege there is a strong psychological component of any plaintiff's complaints. . . . The claim to be initially disputed should be carefully selected. If possible the plaintiff . . . should allege only a nebulous tenosynovitis . . . if the plaintiff can be discredited . . . this would be of considerable significance. Many prospective plaintiffs will treat the first case litigated by the Commonwealth as a 'test case'.[36]

These experiences of accusations of malingering or imagining the symptoms have been common in the UK also. The Hillingdon RSI Support Group was set up in 1986 after two women RSI sufferers approached the Hillingdon Association of Voluntary Services for help. The group discovered that thousands of women were having to deal with intense physical and mental discomfort directly linked to their work, and that GPs, employers and government departments were consistently refusing to take them seriously. Many of the women were nonunionised and in low-paid, low-status jobs.

Michelle Vonahn is a former typesetter and RSI sufferer. She worked for a local authority and had reached speeds of 100 words per minute when she began to experience pain in her forearms and wrists. Her GP diagnosed tenosynovitis and prescribed anti-inflammatory drugs and physiotherapy. But when she returned to work she found male colleagues unsympathetic and office relationships became very strained. Eventually she succeeded in negotiating redeployment but remains angry about her injuries:

> I feel it's just not good enough that women should have to suffer this kind of trauma which affects your personal life as much as meaning you're unable to do the work you're used to. My injury was preventable and I believe trade unions should do more about designing jobs which will avoid RSI,

Tenosynovitis has recently gained publicity through the revelation that Fleet Street journalists, working on new technology, are suffering from it. At the *Financial Times* in particular a number of sub-editors have been unable to continue in their work.[37] And Australian journalists have been discovering the extent of the problem within their profession. In 1987, of the 665 members of the Australian Journalists Association surveyed, 38.5 per cent complained of pain in the arm, 21.1 per cent of loss of strength in the hands or arms, 15.9 per cent of numbness and 12.9 per cent of loss of feeling in the wrists and fingers.[38]

An important victory was won in 1989 when £45,000 was awarded to an RSI victim who had become disabled after working as a secretary at the Midland Bank. Pauline Burnard has had to undergo surgery after the bank delayed changing the height of her desk when she first started suffering pain from typing. Although Midland Bank had admitted negligence and unions said that the settlement would open the way for compensation claims in a range of workplaces, there was no commitment from the employer to change its health and safety policies.[39]

So although this has been something of a breakthrough in terms of gaining recognition of the damage caused by RSI, the equally vital and often more difficult business of influencing companies' health and safety commitments overall remains. At the time of Pauline Burnard's case both the Banking, Insurance and Finance Union and MSF, the general technical union, were actively backing around sixteen cases on behalf of their members which, if successful, could also involve challenging work practices so that RSI is prevented, rather than simply compensated for.

The question of job design is discussed further in chapter 4. Clearly it is crucial to tackle this question if RSI is not to reach epidemic proportions in the office workforce. It can be prevented and, importantly, if it is detected in time permanent injury can be avoided. In its 1988 booklet on RSI, the London Hazards Centre gives detailed guidance on how to recognise RSI and the factors which cause it, and negotiate for improvements that will prevent it occurring in your workplace. Their sample questionnaire is reproduced as a checklist at the end of the chapter.[40] Solutions have to be found in terms of work organisation and equipment design. Repetitive work damages the muscles of your body. Drugs, injections and surgery are no substitute for tackling the problem at source. Try demanding that work be shared so that no one has to stay in the same position all day long. And make sure that no equipment is installed in your office before it has been vetted by those who have to use it.

Remember, safety representatives have this right by law.

Temperature

Being too hot or cold at work seems to have become a regular feature of office life in Britain. There's a lot of talk about the 'greenhouse effect', most of it sounding dire warnings about the damage being done to the world's eco-system. Whatever the real diagnosis, extremes of temperature at unseasonal times of year have meant many people being forced to swelter in offices which can't get their air conditioning working or else shiver on an unexpectedly cold summer's day. There are some legal safeguards to the problem of cold, and by law a thermometer on an unexpectedly cold summer's day. There are some legal. safeguards to the problem of cold, and by law a thermometer must be provided in a conspicuous place on each floor, but not in the case of overheating. The discomforts involved can be equally debilitating along with the increased likelihood of picking up viruses and germs.

The British Institute of Heating and Ventilation Engineers

recommends a minimum temperature of 68°F (20°C) for offices. But under section 6 of the Offices, Shops and Railway Premises Act, only if the temperature in an office falls below 16°C (60.8°F) for more than an hour should a decision be made whether to continue working. The civil service unions have succeeded in negotiating a slightly higher minimum than the statutory one – 65°F (18.5°C). If the heating system fails to produce 65°F and employers don't succeed in quickly restoring the agreed temperature, the unions recommend branches taking appropriate industrial action. In the winter of 1977 the temperature at the London local government office, Brent House, fell below the legal minimum and 400 staff walked out. They came back the following day when management turned up the heating controls and maintained temperatures above the legal minimum from then on.

However, many modern office blocks are also particularly prone to overheating. Factory Inspectorate reports refer to these problems.[41] It is as important to object if you are expected to work in an uncomfortably hot room as much as a cold one.

Modern construction techniques are geared to building office blocks where more workers can be concentrated and work reorganised for efficiency. But tall buildings make wind tunnels, and it may be dangerous to open a window because of severe draughts. So permanent air conditioning, or 'canned air', is a technical necessity. You have to cope with a controlled 'microclimate'.

If the air temperature is too high, your body temperature rises, your heart rate increases and your powers of concentration are reduced. You may get dizzy spells. Exhaustion and drowsiness may follow, which increase the likelihood of accidents. If the temperature is too low, your body loses heat so that you shiver and your muscles and joints become stiff. Your powers of concentration decrease and you become sensitive to even minor draughts. If the humidity is too high, your sweat can't evaporate, thus reducing your body's resistance to high temperatures. If it's too low, your mouth, throat and nose become dry. The upper respiratory tract, with its passages and sinuses, is lined with a mucous membrane which is naturally moist. It acts rather like a moat deterring offensive organisms from entering your body. If it becomes dry even the most geriatric microbes can limp across and begin to multiply.

In a 1987 survey of Kensington and Chelsea town hall offices conducted by NALGO members with the assistance of the London Hazards Centre, over half the workers thought there was usually too little air in the office. Seventy per cent found it too dry and stuffy and virtually all the workers reported that they had no control over the temperature, ventilation, humidity or noise.

Whatever method of heating your employer supplies must be safe.[43] Despite overheating being a serious problem in some offices, there is no statutory maximum temperature limit. However, the Offices, Shops and Railway Premises Act (Sections 6 and 7) does say that employers *must* make *effective* provision for *reasonable temperature and for adequate ventilation* with fresh or purified air. Employers have been prosecuted for failing to do this. Over about 74°F (24°C) your alertness drops and you are more likely to have an accident. 79°F (26°C) is definitely unacceptable.

The increasing use of heat-generating office machinery requires more thought being given to the design and construction of rooms in which these machines are installed. According to the Factory Inspectorate:

One report investigated the complaint of lack of ventilation in a computer room and found temperatures in the range of 29 to 32 degrees C (up to 80°F) not uncommon. Recommended temperature for efficient operation of computers is 21°C (70°F), and the air-conditioning plant which was the only means of ventilation was designed to maintain this temperature in the computer room. Several faults were found and remedied in the air-conditioning plant.

Investigations also showed that similar high temperatures were being recorded in a large room in which data processing machines were being used. The ventilation, which was by means of windows and extractor fans, was found to be inadequate.[44]

And in 1978 secretaries at Aston University walked out of their office when the temperature rose to 80°F due to overheating of the visual display units and other office machinery in the room where they worked.

Use the London Hazards Centre's Action Checklist on temperature:[45]

- Negotiate a maximum and a minimum acceptable temperature before the weather gets too hot or too cold
- Survey 'hot spots' and 'cold spots'; keep a record of temperatures and workers' complaints
- Demand that management have a survey done using the Wet Bulb Globe Temperature Index which takes account of humidity, air movement and workload
- Go for properly designed ventilation or air conditioning. Fans do not cool the air above above 80°F (27°C). Portable air cooling cabinets can reduce air temperature by up to 11°F (6°C)
- Solar gain ('greenhouse effect') from windows can be reduced by reflective film or blinds, and by reducing window area
- An excessively hot or cold workplace is a hazard: don't stay in it.

Ventilation

The most common complaint voiced by office workers is poor ventilation. A recent Harris Poll found that more than two-thirds of the working population of London believe that their productivity could improve in a working environment with cleaner and fresher air. Seventy-nine per cent of those questioned complained that the air where they worked was stuffy or stale.[46] Many large employers are expanding their copying and duplicating departments piecemeal until they become full-scale printshops, housed in totally unsuitable basement rooms, where the ventilation was not designed to deal with the resulting air pollution. The severity and extent of ventilation problems have been greatly underestimated. If you're working in a poorly ventilated environment forty hours a week, year after year, these conditions are irritating, stressful and dangerous to your health.

The chemicals commonly used in offices and emitted by photocopiers, laser printers and other reproduction equipment mean that good ventilation is absolutely essential for your health. Heating systems can also pump out carbon monoxide.

- In an accounts firm housed in a multi-occupancy building, the staff complained of severe headaches, particularly in cold weather. Rather than its being due to bad ventilation, as originally thought, it was found to be caused by high levels of carbon monoxide coming from a residential flat below the office heated by a gas-fire boiler.

- Peter Wilson fainted while filing computer paper in the Hammersmith and Fulham town hall. The doctor at the hospital he was taken to diagnosed his collapse as due to inadequate ventilation.[47]

There are two kinds of ventilation: general, which is air conditioning, and exhaust, which removes dust or fumes from a hazardous process. Air conditioning distributes fresh air throughout the building at a comfortable temperature and humidity. But it's not very effective in controlling hazardous substances since it merely relies on fresh air to dilute such substances.

A wall-mounted fan isn't the same as general ventilation. The most a fan can do is suck some cigarette smoke and air-borne germs across the room and out of the window. Ventilation from another room is not good enough either. Clean, fresh air is a vital requirement for healthy working conditions.[48]

Office workers in Kensington and Chelsea Council offices moved into the new town hall building in 1978. Immediately, they began to complain of very dry air and breathing difficulties, many sore throats and an increase in the number of colds and 'flu. Workers who wore contact lenses suffered from eye irritation due to the dry air. NALGO departmental reps communicated these complaints to management and health and safety inspectors. NALGO members voted to have a walk-out once a week at 4 p.m. as long as was necessary to get something done. The Council then agreed to install a humidifying system. As part of their cutback in public expenditure, the Council had removed humidification in the air-conditioning plant to save £40,000. To install the system would now cost them a lot more.

However, dry air was not the only problem suffered by these workers. Laurie Lopes started work at the town hall in January 1979 and was surprised to see a worker watering the carpets. 'Static', she was told. A subsequent survey conducted by NALGO in 1987 confirmed a host of symptoms experienced by staff which can be found in similar air-conditioned, sealed buildings. This has been called the 'sick building syndrome' which is defined by the World Health Organisation as general, non-specific symptoms of malaise, in particular irritation of nose, throat and eyes, lethargy and headaches, experienced at work but ceasing shortly afterwards.

Survey results

Symptom	% *usually or always suffering the symptom at work*
Stuffy nose	42
Skin dryness	41
Lethargy	40
Headaches	30
Eye irritation	30
Throat irritation	30

Laurie, who subsequently became NALGO branch secretary, described their struggle to convince management of the serious extent of the health hazards facing the staff thus:

It is typical of our management's uncaring attitude that genuine concerns have been dismissed as 'imagined' or 'hysterical'. All we get are repeated assurances that there's no problem. But now our survey has clearly demonstrated that persistent symptoms of lethargy, itchy eyes, dry skin and sore throats are the result of an unhealthy workplace, not fertile imaginations. We will use these findings to insist management improve the woeful office heating, lighting and ventilation, deal with the real cause of our ill-health and give us some control over the working environment.[49]

Similar difficulties faced the all-female staff at Milton Keynes Jobcentre, which opened in 1980. A distinctive feature of their working days was the 'three o'clock flush' – a reddening of the face which many experienced along with chest problems, sinusitis and a general lethargy. In 1984, the staff organised through their union, the CPSA, for solutions. They demanded an independent review, and over the next two years struggled with management's piecemeal palliatives. At one point a contractor doing repair work on the building claimed: 'That bunch of women are always complaining about something, there's nothing wrong with the building.' Eventually the Manpower Services Commission's deputy safety officer carried out a safety audit which tallied exactly with the union's and a survey was commissioned from Dr Alan Dunn of the South Bank Polytechnic. Poor ventilation, glass fibres polluting the air, high humidity, bad lighting and glare were all discovered. Management have now spent £30,000 on improving the working environment and the sickness level has dropped dramatically. As Cathy Pearce, the branch secretary, said:

The struggle to improve conditions in Milton Keynes led to contacts with trade union branches fighting similar 'sick building' problems in the civil service. We are trying to help sort out ventilation problems for Luton and Colchester Job Centres – where managers turned the ventilation systems off because they were too noisy – the DHSS tower block in Milton Keynes and a job centre in Kilmarnock. Our fight has shown members in the office that it is possible to improve their working environment if they unite and do not simply accept what management says.[50]

At a fringe health and safety meeting during its 1984 conference, NALGO was alerted to the possibility of a link between ill health and the buildings in which their members worked. In 1988, the union's national health and safety committee said it 'had to face many accusations of hysteria and over-reaction and . . . welcomes the publication by the Health and Safety Executive of a special inspector's report which acknowledges there is a problem.'[51]

In the USA this type of health hazard is referred to as 'tight building syndrome' and it was estimated (in 1984) that as many as 30 per cent of the requests to the National Institute for Occupational Safety and Health (NIOSH) for health hazard evaluations were from office workers in sealed buildings.[52]

Wherever dust or fumes exist, exhaust ventilation is essential. Some of the strongest words in health and safety legislation relate to this problem:

> Effective and suitable provision shall be made for securing and maintaining, by the circulation of adequate supplies of fresh or artificially purified air, the ventilation of every room comprised in or constituting premises to which this Act applies.[53]

This is not weakened by the words 'as far as reasonably practicable'. The duty on the employer is clear, although it may require a bit of pushing from you.

Ventilation itself can be hazardous. It can redistribute polluted air round the building instead of cleaning it; it can emit stale air into the corridor; it can be noisy. All of these faults can be rectified.

Draughts too are a common complaint in offices.They can cause aching muscles and stress. An efficient general ventilation system replaces the air removed by the exhaust system and distributes it evenly throughout the office so that cross-draughts are avoided.

Some air conditioning systems use ozone to sweeten the air and mask smells. Ozone, even in minute quantities, irritates the mucous membranes, causes sore throats and can harm the lungs. It doesn't neutralise smells, it masks them. Be careful of ioniser air conditioners as some emit ozone.

A new occupational disease, 'secretary's asthma' or 'humidifier fever', has been caused by air conditioning which humidifies the air. The symptoms include intermittent chills and fever, coughing, vomiting, aching joints and tightness in the chest. It has been dismissed by some managers as 'just a bug' or malingering. An article in *The Observer* (31 December 1978) discussed the likelihood of amoeba breeding in the water reservoirs of air conditioners causing 'flu or even fibrosis of the lung. Recent outbreaks of legionnaire's disease have been traced to the water tanks of air conditioning systems. Deaths at the BBC's Portland

Place building and as a result of contact with a system at Leicester Square during 1989 have led to local authorities setting up environmental health units to monitor air conditioning systems, checking for *legionella* and instigating clean-ups.

If you demand a survey of the air in your office a machine may be used which measures thermal comfort, to assess such things as the face temperature of the skin. This is called the 'comfy test'. It's okay as far as it goes, but it's also important to ask people how they *feel* and whether there's been a noticeable increase in colds, for instance.

If you want a ventilation system where the windows can be opened, management may confront you with the 'security' argument. Often, says an annual Factory Inspectorate report done in 1971, 'windows are nailed permanently shut, or even bricked up'. Legislation demands that ventilation be provided and such criminal activity on the part of employers should not be tolerated.

Much research on air conditioning and ventilation is done because it promotes 'worker efficiency' and 'higher productivity'. A fortunate by-product is that it also promotes health. But in preparing your case for better air conditioning systems you can always point out that you'll all be more alert and contented in a more comfortable environment. What is more, computers stop working if the air conditioning is of a poor standard. Some office workers might too.

Dangerous Substances: Chemicals, Gases and Dusts

In offices, especially, employees run the risk of exposure to harmful products of which often they do not realise the danger.[54]

More than one million substances are used in workplaces in Britain and new ones are being introduced every day:[55] 2400 of them are suspected of causing cancer. Office workers use many chemicals in the form of powders, liquids or in aerosols. Some machinery gives off harmful gases, and the air in offices is polluted with dust from insulation and ventilation systems.

However, Regulation 7 of the new Control of Substances Hazardous to Health Regulations 1988 imposes a clear duty on employers to ensure that the exposure of their employees to hazardous substances is either prevented or 'where this is not reasonably practicable', adequately controlled.

Substances such as typewriter cleaning and correcting fluids, used daily by typists in small quantities, may contain, among others, the toxin trichloroethane. If some is spilled toxic fumes can reach dangerously high levels. The long-term effect of exposure to small quantities of many of these substances is untested and unknown. The number of chemicals in use that do *not* have to be tested under the Notification of New Substances Regulations 1982 has been fixed at 107,000. The Chemical Industry Association admit that they have no toxicity information on the long-term effects of 75 per cent of these substances.

Chemical substances enter the human body via a number of routes. As fumes or dusts, they can be inhaled, irritating the lungs and entering the bloodstream, from where they may affect other organs. In any form they can cause dermatitis (irritation of the skin) and possibly skin cancer after prolonged exposure. Or if you are eating or drinking, and there are fumes or dust in the air, you may be ingesting chemicals via your digestive system.

If you come in contact with a chemical, your body may react to it immediately. This is known as an *acute* reaction, and it is usually easy to trace the cause. At other times you may work with a chemical substance for years and slowly become sensitised to it. This is known as a *chronic* reaction. Asbestos, for example, can cause cancer *twenty years* after exposure. When this happens, it is often difficult to trace the cause, since a minute quantity of the chemical concerned may cause the reaction and it could be something present at work or at home.

Acceptable Levels

The government has set standards for some dangerous chemicals which are known as occupational exposure limits (OELs). In its 1989 Guidance Note[56] the Health and Safety Executive (HSE) defines the two kinds of OEL currently in use:

The Maximum Exposure Limit (MEL) is the maximum concentration of an airborne substance (averaged over a reference period) to which employees may be exposed by inhalation under any circumstances.

An Occupational Exposure Standard (OES) is the concentration of an airborne substance (averaged over a reference period) at which, according to current knowledge, there is no evidence that it is likely to be injurious to employees if they are exposed by inhalation, day after day.

The HSE itself admits that OESs for chemicals are approved even when only limited scientific data are available. Often little is known about the long-term or carcinogenic effects. The calculations are based on what is 'safe' for the 'average worker', who is a male and generally heavier and carrying less fat than a woman. Little account is taken of the effects of exposure to more than one chemical, or a 'cocktail' of chemicals at a time. Hazards Centres (see Appendix III) advise that chemicals should be treated as hazardous until proven safe – not the other way around.

In 1989 the Control of Substances Hazardous to Health Regulations (COSHH regs) placed a number of important additional duties on employers. They must:

1 make a *written assessment* of the hazards caused by all the substances used in their workplace;
2 provide safety reps with copies of the assessment and of the list of substances used and their hazards (the 'substances audit' with 'data sheets' from the suppliers or manufacturers);
3 measure the workplace air for contamination by dust, fumes, etc. (this is called 'environmental monitoring' and should be carried out by competent 'occupational hygienists');
4 keep all exposures of workers to hazardous substances as low as possible, and certainly well below the published 'exposure limits';
5 use engineering controls and improved work methods, materials and processes to reduce exposure to dust and fumes, rather than putting workers in respirators;
6 provide medical check-ups;
7 provide adequate information, instruction, training and supervision;
8 involve safety reps by giving them copies of the results of measuring the workplace air and by consulting them about the introduction of new substances, the control of existing ones, the kind of medical surveillance needed.

Common Chemicals in Offices

Correcting fluids are usually solvent-based and can injure your skin, liver and brain. *Tippex*, for instance, contains 1,1,1 tri-chloroethane. According to a report for the US Department of Health, Education and Welfare National Institute of Occupational Safety and Health, this can cause, in humans:

headaches, dizziness, slowness, sleepiness, weakness, ringing sound in ears, prickling sensation in hands and feet, liver damage, sickness, vomiting, diarrhoea, drop in blood pressure, slower heart rate, dry and cracked or inflamed skin, eye irritation.[57]

Snopake contains titanium resin and toluene which is reported to cause eye, skin and throat irritation. Toluene is used by glue sniffers. Roneo stencil correcting fluid contains methylated spirit, acetone, ether and dibutylphthalate, which are generally irritants to the eyes, throat and skin.

Water-based correcting fluids are much safer and *Tippex* correction paper is harmless. You may only be working with small quantities of the substance but you may also be exposed to them all your working life.

Self-copying paper has been identified as hazardous by the National Board of Occupational Safety and Health in Finland. As long ago as 1977 they issued a circular pointing out that it can cause skin allergies. In 1976 office workers at the Inner London Education Authority who were handling self-copying forms suffered an outbreak of catarrh, headaches and coughing. The forms were coated with a plastic containing dye and solvent which burst on contact, making a copy but also releasing a fine dust which got into the eyes, nose and throat. Following complaints from staff, ILEA changed to a mechanical transfer type of self-copying paper which has a pigment layer on the back. Staff subsequently found they no longer experienced these illnesses.

Electrostencil machines emit carbon dust and poisonous gases. These can act like a chemical 'cocktail' that is not covered by the occupational exposure limits, which set limits for individual chemicals. The most important safety precaution for these machines is adequate ventilation. The manufacturer Roneo-Vickers recommends 'a minimum of four room air changes an hour . . . as high as ten changes per hour [is] preferable'.[58]

Photocopiers, if used occasionally, are fairly safe. But those workers whose main or major part of their daily tasks is photocopying may find themselves suffering dermatitis, bronchial complaints, dry eyes, nose and throat. The greatest source of these health dangers is the emission of ozone and the chemical contained in toners.

Ozone is a gas produced by high voltage electrical equipment;

it is sweet smelling and highly toxic. The OEL is one part in ten million parts of air. *If you can smell it, the level is too high.* As Ralph Nader points out: 'The long-range effects of ozone exposure show that ozone can significantly alter the structure of cells and tissues, most importantly in the lungs.'[59] A New Zealand study carried out in 1981 by the Central Occupational Health Unit of the Department of Health showed eye discomfort and upper respiratory tract irritation consistently experienced by people using photocopiers and not by a control group of workers used in comparison who had no association with photocopying machines. Photocopiers in frequent use must have good quality exhaust ventilation fitted to ensure safe, clean air.

Dangerous Substances in the Office Building

Many offices, in both the public and private sectors, are partly constructed of asbestos. Traditionally it has been used as insulation in partitions, pipe lagging and cable ducts. Asbestos is a known killer. In Britain it has been estimated that more than half a million workers may die due to asbestos-related diseases in the next thirty years.[60]

In 1987, the new *Control of Asbestos at Work Regulations* were introduced which are meant to provide protection for everyone at work who could be at risk from exposure to asbestos, not just those in asbestos manufacturing or high-risk jobs.

Also in 1987, the Health and Safety Executive's confirmation of the cancer hazards of mineral fibres[61] coincided with the successful conclusion of two years' negotiation between the National Communications Union and British Telecom over the health hazards of mineral fibres.[62] The agreement includes a restriction on the use of man-made mineral fibre boards which release fibres that can be inhaled.

Dust in filing rooms can give you a sore throat. The overall exposure limit on *any* dust has been set at a maximum of 10 mg per cubic metre total dust concentration in the air or 5 mg per cubic metre of 'respirable' dust concentration in the air.[63]

How damaging the dusts are depends on the size of the particle or fibre, the type of dust, and the quantity you are exposed to. You are more at risk if you breathe in dust over months and years. But dust-related cancers do *not* depend on how much you breathe in; one tiny fibre can cause the disease.

Glass fibre, Rockwool and other brand-named insulation materials (often known as man-made mineral fibres) present some of the same problems as asbestos. They too are constructed from tiny fibres which can be inhaled and have been found to cause lung cancer. Glass fibre can cause severe skin irritation or dermatitis.

Office building materials themselves can emit toxic fumes as the following example shows.

During 1989, workers in 'Yorkon Demountable' prefabricated offices in Greenwich suffered from dizziness, chest infections, headaches and breathing problems. An air test demanded by their union, NALGO, identified three highly toxic chemicals – methyl isobutyl ketone, xylene and styrene – which appeared to be emitted from the cavity filling in the exterior walls. The union asked for a full independent survey, to be paid by the employer, and threatened to leave the building if it was not carried out.[64]

Most office furniture is made of chipboard. The resin which bonds the wood chips together is urea formaldehyde. Formaldehyde is a powerful irritant to eyes, nose and throat at concentrations below the maximum exposure limit of 2 parts per million (ppm). It is a common cause of allergic skin rashes and asthma, and is a probable human carcinogen. In a modern, sealed office with inadequate ventilation, formaldehyde emissions can easily reach irritant levels.

Twenty-one office workers in a mobile trailer were exposed to formaldehyde fumes from resin-containing chipboard flooring and plywood panelling. The levels were between 0.12 and 0.16ppm (nearly 20 times less than the maximum exposure limit). The workers had a marked increase in headaches and tiredness as well as chest tightness.[65]

Whether it is chemicals in regular use in the office, or stored and dangerous ones that can leak, catch fire or explode, whether it is levels of dust in the air or pollution from outside the building being breathed in for eight hours a day, office workers should feel empowered to question management assurances that there are no health hazards. New machines can introduce new hazards, so demand full information first rather than waiting until workers start getting headaches, skin rashes, bronchitis, etc. It's not good enough to be told by your boss to 'take care' when handling chemicals. If you're breathing in the stuff forty hours a week there could be a slow build-up of health damage. It's up to your employer to safeguard you against this and no amount of research denying the hazards should succeed in deterring you if people are reporting worrying symptoms.

The Basics: Welfare Facilities and Hygiene

Offices vary in the welfare amenities provided for the people who work in them. Some are grim dirty places, with only minimum amenities. Others are spacious and bright. But many offices, both old and new, leave much to be desired.

Fiona McNally worked as a temp at the 'XYZ Credit Company'. She described her workplace:

> The firm occupied the eighth floor of a large, modern office block . . . . The locus of higher management was adorned by wall-to-wall carpets and elegant furnishings, that of lower management by fairly stylish fittings and bright paintwork, whereas the filing department, where I was to be employed, was a barren wasteland of rickety chairs and tables, with not so much as a calendar to grace the fading, dirty walls. This enormous room was dominated by tall, rusty filing cabinets which effectively prevented the sunshine from entering.[66]

The Office, Shops and Railway Premises Act (OSRPA) sets down some specific minimum requirements, and you will probably have to fight to get more. But beware! One book written for management gives the following guidelines:

> In providing amenities, any suggestion of paternalism or generosity should be avoided. 'We like you to have the best conditions to get from you the best work' is not only a realistic approach, but one that breeds confidence.[67]

Space

Each person should have at least 11.3 cubic metres with 3.7 square metres (40 square feet) of floor space. The space occupied by workers' furniture is ignored, but space taken up by other equipment, filing cabinets or machinery is subtracted from the space. Your employer has a legal duty to provide this.[68] Where the ceiling is lower than 3 metres (10 feet), at least 11 cubic metres (400 cubic feet) per person must be allowed. 3.7 square metres (40 square feet) isn't much. Standards as usual vary for what is deemed a basic minimum. In Ireland the minimum is 4.6 square metres (50 square feet), and the International Labour Office recommends 7 to 8.4 square metres (75 to 90 square feet) per worker. A British government inquiry into conditions in the Civil Service recommends 5.6 square metres (60 square feet) for a clerical worker and 3.7 square metres (40 square feet) for a typist.

An overcrowded office is a health hazard. It means more risk of injury, more stress, less light and increased risk of infection. Lack of space means desks and filing cabinets become obstructions, causing bumps and bruises. Adequate working space round office machinery is essential to enable adjustment, repairs and cleaning to be carried out safely.

In spite of the legal requirements, offices are still overcrowded. In one Ministry of Defence building in south London, 160 office staff are currently working in three converted corridors. The Factory Inspectorate had occasion to prosecute a firm employing hundreds of clerks: 37 persons were working where the permitted number was 23, and 17 other offices occupied by the firm were found to be overcrowded.[69] Overcrowding can occur in both old and new offices. Employing temps at peak work periods can create serious overcrowding problems because sufficient space has not been created. In a 1988 City Centre Survey of 600 VDU workers, 55 per cent of respondents reported problems of overcrowding and most complained that their offices were poorly planned and laid out.[70]

Typists are often crowded in the 'pool', but you'll rarely see an overcrowded manager's office. Often, the higher the concentration of women in a particular area of the office, the lower the standard of decor and the less space for each individual. The 'mixed' areas are next. And the smartest are usually the men-only bastion (boardroom, executive lounge). Women tend to receive the same proportion of office space as they do of pay: 20–50 per cent less than men. Space is officially allocated according to status and not health and safety. Have you ever been asked how much space you need to work in? Or whether you prefer open plan or partitioned offices? An interesting theory is put forward by Rosemary Pringle[71] about certain crucial characteristics which distinguish 'men's work' and 'women's work'. Linked to an understanding of masculinity as involving an active, controlling relation to the world, she argues that men are allowed more space and mobility at work. The sorts of job commonly perceived as 'men's' and usually occupied by them entail the worker in moving around the workplace, whether to investigate situations, issue orders or operate machinery which requires large, expansive movements. Women, on the other hand, are expected to sit in small, confined places making restricted movements and waiting for work to come to them. This physical limitation on the amount of space they occupy or are expected to move through is directly linked to the amount of control they have over their work and decision-making. The more power you have at work, the 'bigger' a person you are seen to be and so your movements become less closely supervised. In this way men can be seen as adults at work and women as children or 'girls' – as they are usually called, even when heading for retirement age. As one GLC typist, who worked in one of a number of crowded typing rooms, put it: 'It's like being at school here, you even have to ask to go to the toilet. We're grown women and yet we get treated like naughty schoolgirls half the time who can't be trusted to get on with their work.'

Open Plan Offices

Open plan offices can cause problems: individual requirements for air and warmth vary, and there's noise from telephones and machines. A related problem is smoking and the dangers of passive smoking (breathing in other people's smoke), which have now been documented.[72]

The management philosophy behind the open plan office is that it ensures uniform work with no slacking, since it's harder to talk or read in the open than in the privacy of a separate room. Open plan makes for easier supervision. Offices are sometimes partitioned as an afterthought. An inspector states:

It is when offices are inspected after partitioning that interior offices with screens extending to ceiling height are sometimes found to be without ventilation, with borrowed natural lighting and often overcrowded.[73]

Developers of high-rise office blocks cannot estimate the number of people likely to be employed in the premises, so they often fail to provide sufficient amenities such as washing facilities. Such problems could be reduced if office buildings were designed for flexibility, taking into account the needs of those who have to work in them. Offices should be open plan only if *you* want them to be. They could be re-organised, with open plan areas together with a 'thinking room' and a 'reading room' which people could share and use when necessary.

Washing and Toilet Facilities

At the Bexley Heath office of the Pearl Assurance Company office workers refused to merge with another office unless more toilets were installed. Four women and three men worked in the office, sharing one toilet with fifteen agents who also regularly used the office. The ASTMS (now MSF) branch secretary pressed the public health inspector to issue an Improvement Notice, which he did, although Pearl appealed. After a great deal of union pressure Pearl agreed to build new sanitary facilities. Pearl repeatedly said they couldn't afford to spend the necessary £20,000. (At the same time they were spending £80,000 on an advertising campaign.) The branch secretary said staff would soon have decent toilet and eating facilities – but only after eighteen months 'of bitter struggle'. He personally believes that other Pearl offices are probably contravening the Offices and Shops Act on requirement of toilet facilities.[74]

There is a statutory requirement to provide at least one lavatory for every 25 people.[75] If there are more than ten women workers, there must be suitable and effective means for disposal of sanitary towels. Like all the legal standards, this is a basic minimum – and a pathetic one at that. There should be towel or tampon vending machines, although there is no legal requirement for this. Lavatories must be conveniently accessible and they must be clean, private and well ventilated, by law. Detailed requirements for toilet facilities are outlined in the Sanitary Convenience Regulations 1964.

There must be a supply of clean, running, hot and cold water. Soap and clean towels (or their equivalent) must be provided and kept clean. There must be at least one basin for 15 workers.[76] Separate lavatories and washing facilities for men and women must be provided if more than five people are employed. Many office workers' sanitary facilities are still a disgrace, with broken washbasins and mirrors and inadequate standards of cleanliness and lighting. Most employers only provide the minimum, or less.

Cloakrooms

Provision of suitable and adequate cloakroom space for clothing not worn during working hours is the employer's statutory duty, under section 12 of OSRPA. Nails on the wall don't make a cloakroom. Ideally, you'll want space for changing footwear. Space for drying outdoor clothing should also be provided. Have a look at your boss's facilities – this will be a good guideline for the kind of standard to aim for.

Eating and Drinking Facilities

Wholesome drinking water must be in plentiful supply. The regulations for this are often met by fitting taps over water basins in the washrooms. 'This', said London's Chief Public Health Inspector 'is potentially dangerous and aesthetically unacceptable.' If there is no piped supply, the water store must be changed daily. A means of drinking the water must be provided, either by cups or drinking fountains.[77]

Where meals are eaten on the premises in offices and shops there must be 'suitable and sufficient' places for eating.[78] Even where there are no specific regulations. The *Health and Safety at Work Act 1974* requires all employers to make adequate

arrangements for the welfare of employees. Ideally, in any size-able organisation, the employer should provide a canteen with good food at reasonable prices. A rest room where workers can take their breaks and prepare a meal or a hot drink should be the minimum.[79]

Some employers supply tea and coffee by machine, but these frequently break down, the drinks are far from wholesome and some office workers are now refusing to use them since the drinks have been found to cause chronic constipation.

Discoveries of the dangers of food poisoning (salmonella and listeria) in much of the food we eat, particularly convenience food, provide a powerful case for high standards of health and hygiene to be met in any staff-catering facilities. There are some simple precautions regarding storage and cooking of food which are important to follow if staff are to avoid being poisoned by their own canteen. If you feel that this has not been recognised by your catering management, start asking questions; don't wait for the office to fall sick. If in doubt, contact your local author-ity's Environmental Health Department.

Microwave Ovens

Microwave ovens are now in use in many pubs, canteens, res-taurants and private homes. The manufacturers claim that microwave radiation which heats the food is contained within the glass and metal case of the oven. All ovens are fitted with automatic locks which are supposed to switch off the radiation as soon as the door is opened or even if the door is not firmly shut because of the build-up of grease or dirt. The British Stan-dards Institution specifies that the radiation level emitted should be not more than $5mW/cm^2$ (5 milliwatts per square centimetre) at a distance of 2 inches from the door of the oven.

Many normally functioning ovens without faults have been found to leak microwave radiation, while in use, at *levels above the $5mW/cm^2$* standard. Indeed, after one survey, the American Consumers Union refused to recommend as safe *any* model of microwave oven.

Over-exposure to the electromagnetic energy from microwave ovens may cause a heating effect on the skin and other tissues which is not felt as a burning sensation, but which affects sensi-tive organs like the eyes, the genitals and the abdomen. There is some (as yet inconclusive) evidence that this may result in eye cataracts, sterilisation, birth deformities, hereditary damage, and nervous system and blood disorders. To ensure that you are not exposed to the harmful effects of microwaves in your workplace, use the following GMB checklist:

1 Has the oven been manufactured to the latest British Standards Institution recommendations?
2 Is the oven fitted with two oven door interlocks that prevent the oven working when the door is not fully closed?
3 Is the oven sited well away from where workers are seated?
4 Is the oven cleaned daily so that spillage does not stop the door from closing properly?
5 Is the oven regularly maintained and checked for radiation leakage every six months?
6 Are the manufacturers'/suppliers' instructions on maintenance followed?
7 Is the leakage of radiation measured by competent people using accurate instruments? (The inspector from the local authority Environmental Health Department is equipped for such tests and will do free surveys if they consider it a priority.)
8 Are all leaks well below the control limit of $5mW/cm^2$ at 5 cm from the oven?
9 Is there any obvious damage to the joints, door or any other parts of the oven? If so, then a further leakage test will be necessary.
10 Is the oven checked for electrical faults and kept in good working order?
11 Canned food, or anything that has a non-porous casing, should not be warmed in a microwave oven, because of the build-up of pressure that will be released when the object is punctured.[80]

Cleanliness

All premises, furniture and fittings are required by law to be kept in a clean state.[81] Dirt and refuse must not be allowed to accumulate, and floors and steps must be washed or, if appropriate, swept at least once a week.

Insect infestations are an increasing problem in modern offices where the warm heating ducts, hollow walls, floors and poor standards of cleaning create an ideal environment for insects to thrive.

Monthly spraying of one poorly cleaned office led to a build-up of pesticide-laden dust but workers were still being bitten. The union branch (MSF) successfully demanded proper cleaning, since when there have been no further reports of bites. The pests were never identified and the pesticide company admitted their product was being misused. Cleaning and identification should have been the first steps.[82]

Indiscriminate treatment with highly toxic pesticides is often carried out in preference to eliminating the conditions which allow infestation. Use the London Hazards Centre's factsheets on insect infestations to help find a safe solution if you have this problem in your workplace.[83]

Some office workers complain of skin rashes resulting from dirt and dust at their workplace. There are stories of vermin, rats and mice residing in offices. The spread of infection, including dermatitis, and colds and 'flu, is often compounded by unhygienic toilets, washrooms, cooking and eating facilities.

In many cases management employs contract cleaners who usually work at night or very early in the morning and have to clean huge blocks. They're often unable to do the job properly. They may not be contracted to clean storerooms, cupboards or eating facilities. It is better to employ permanent cleaners to do a thorough job. Try to contact the cleaners and, if possible, link up with them on health and safety.

There is some evidence that the incidence of sickness diminishes notably if telephones and intercommunication equipment are regularly disinfected.[84]

Decoration

In addition to cleanliness, comfort and colour are also important. Bright and pleasant surroundings affect your morale and your mental health. Yet often it's only the area which is open to the public – the reception area – which is well furnished and pleasantly decorated. The drab office that can't be changed by any amount of effort (for example, plants and pictures) is depressing. But possibly more of a strain in some ways is the glossy, decorated office which is not allowed to bear any sign of the personalities of those who work there.

In May 1926, W. Keay, General Secretary of the National Federation of Professional Workers, wrote:

It may come as a surprise to many that in several of the public services the conditions are nearly as deplorable as in offices under private control. People, when speaking of, for example, the Civil Service, think of the front rooms in Whitehall and are more or less unacquainted with the miserable, damp, unhealthy accommodation frequently accorded to, say, customs officers at the Ports, or the sickly, dark kennels, in which many of those engaged in Inland Revenue duties and in the work of Labour Exchanges throughout the provinces have to spend their working hours. Cuts in expenditure on such services have been secured in several instances by the maintenance of premises never intended for permanent habitation.[85]

This from one of the thousands of leaflets written in the fifty years of trade union campaigning to obtain protective legislation for offices.

There is little doubt that following the passing of the Office, Shops and Railway Premises Act in 1963 standards have improved. But many office workers still work in damp basements, windowless rooms, converted warehouses and corridors. In the public sector, many clerical staff work in appalling conditions which are a result of the cuts in public expenditure – a feature of life now as in 1926.

In October 1980 an edict went out from the Property Services Agency (part of the Department of the Environment) forbidding redecoration of government buildings. *The only exception to this cutback in public expenditure was where redecoration was necessary for health and safety reasons.*

Rest Rooms and First Aid Facilities

A first aid box or cupboard containing only first aid requisites must be provided for the use of all employees and be readily accessible. The Health and Safety (First Aid) Regulations 1981 set out the minimum required number of first aiders.

Even the smallest workplace must have at least one person who has been formally appointed to take charge if someone is injured or becomes ill at work. Appointed persons should:

- Be trained in emergency first aid
- Know how to take charge in an emergency
- Keep first aid facilities in good order

At least one trained first aider is required in any workplace, however low the risk, if there are 150 or more employees. With more than 400 employees there should also be a first aid room. These apply to workplaces where there are no occupational health services.

However, as pointed out in *Bargaining Report*[86], according to a previous survey of over 400 companies done in 1982 at the time the Regulations came into effect, some workplaces had more first aiders than were set out in the approved code. The law should be seen as providing a basic minimum requirement and preferable standards negotiated for.[87]

There is a worrying get-out clause for employers under the new regulations which allows the Health and Safety Executive to 'exempt any person or class of persons from any of the requirements imposed by these regulations'. Trade union pressure should seek to get this clause repealed if workers are to be assured of an acceptable provision of first aid facilities.

Under the Act first aiders are allowed time off work with pay for training and any duties they need to perform. However, in workplaces where there are difficulties in recruiting first aiders, arguably there needs also to be a weekly allowance paid to staff who take on these responsibilities. A survey of 657 workplaces done by the HSE[88] five years after the regulations came into force highlights some appalling inadequacies.[89] Four out of ten workplaces did not have a qualified first aider. Of those that did, one in three had only one, so there was no cover if that person was absent. Two hundred and twenty-four companies had chemical hazards on the premises but 92 per cent had no one trained to deal with chemical accidents. Only one in five had a first aid box and in half of these it was inaccessible. Deirdre Hunt, a file clerk in a plastics firm, reported that the manager kept the key to the first-aid box, which was locked in his room. In one large bank, the box held nothing but a rusty screw.

The Inner London Education Authority (before it was abolished) paid trained office first aiders an additional £50 a year. There are companies which pay people to take on this responsibility and this is certainly something to push for in your workplace. There should also be a first aid room or rest room with a sofa or comfortable chair where you can go if injured or feeling unwell. Rest rooms are especially important for pregnant workers and women with menstrual cramps. The lack of legislation for this should not deter you from arguing for it.

An assembly control clerk working for Lucas Electrical described the paltry facilities at her factory:

> If you're feeling rough and need to sit down you've got the choice of a hard plastic seat in the staff canteen or the toilet where there's a broken wooden chair. It's like they just expect us to soldier on however we feel. Women getting period pains is not something that male managers can be bothered about. It's stupid really because we'd work better and wouldn't be forced to take whole days off if they gave us a proper rest room.[90]

For those workers who are operating a VDU and who have got a new technology agreement which stipulates regular breaks from VDU work, a designated room to take these breaks in would help make it much more likely that the agreement would be adhered to. (See chapter 4.) If you've got nowhere to go except the corridor, and the pressure of work is intense, nine times out of ten you're likely to carry on keying in and hurting your eyes, running the risk of gynaecological problems and increasing headaches.

Some rooms are worse than useless. One first aid room in a customs and excise office in the south-east has kitchen stores in it which require open windows; the result is a cold, draughty rest room. Many have nothing in the medical cupboard and no toilet. Another, in a large government building, is a total shambles, full of stored furniture, and next to the kitchen so that the sick feel sicker from the smell of cooking food.

It is essential that a record is kept of all first aid cases treated, preferably in the accident book kept alongside the first aid box. Such records can be used to identify particularly hazardous areas so that preventive measures can be taken.

All workplaces with more than ten employees must have an accident book where details of all accidents can be recorded by the employee concerned, or by someone on their behalf. The book should also be used to record any sickness possibly caused by work as well as dangerous occurrences or 'near-misses' in the workplace.

Childcare at Work

Many office workers are parents. Childcare during working hours can be a desperate problem and affects a worker's welfare. In this society childcare is seen as the responsibility of the mother, and working mothers often have to carry this heavy burden alone. The deeply unhelpful attitude of some employers is illustrated by a case taken to an Industrial Tribunal by Cathy Burke, a SOGAT member at the *Daily Mail*, in 1987. She was given a verbal disciplinary warning for 'unauthorised absence' when she needed to collect her child from nursery after being told her childminder couldn't do it. She'd requested 1¾ hours' unpaid leave that she would make up later but was refused. Eventually she took 50 minutes off and brought her child to the chapel office until her holiday began in the afternoon. Just before the Industrial Tribunal was to begin her employer agreed a settlement which allowed staff to take time for emergencies such as a breakdown in childcare arrangements. No doubt if Cathy Burke had not taken the case to a Tribunal this important improvement would not have been gained.[91]

Very few employers provide workplace nurseries. In 1975 there were only 90 in Britain, most of which were in hospitals or academic institutions. Fourteen years later, in 1989, there were still only 100 workplace nurseries, mostly in the public sector, giving Britain one of the worst records in Europe. Only one per cent of under fives have places in local authority day nurseries and ten per cent in nursery classes or schools.[92] As Bronwen Cohen points out in her comprehensive survey of childcare provision, *Caring for Children: Services and Policies for Childcare and Equal Opportunities in the UK*,[93] the government keeps no statistics on workplace nurseries, seeing it as a matter solely between employer and employees.

Added to this has been the punitive tax situation for anybody using a workplace nursery and earning over £8500. Parents were taxed on any subsidy provided by the employer and so faced enormously high costs. The government finally succumbed to consistent pressure in the 1990 Finance Bill ('Budget') to change this and put workplace nurseries in the same category as subsidised staff canteens.

The Workplace Nurseries Campaign has produced a useful information pack[94] for groups negotiating for better workplace childcare provision and the Childcare Now campaign organises for improvements in all aspects of childcare provision for under fives.[95]

The London Borough of Camden's staff nursery is administered by a committee of parents, union and management. But places are like gold dust. As one woman about to return to work after having her second child put it:

> I was contacted last week because they've finally got a place to offer me for my first son. I had to laugh because three years later there's the baby who needs looking after too. So there's no way I'll be able to take the place and ferry the two of them to different places each morning.

One example of a workplace nursery is Bridgewater Square Nursery at the Barbican, London, which is two-thirds funded by the merchant bank Merrill Lynch. The local authority, the London Borough of Islington, succeeding in getting it set up by making it a condition of planning permission to develop the bank's office. It is run by City Child, an organisation set up to develop and manage daycare facilities for under fives whose parents live or work in the City. Priority is given to employees of Merrill Lynch.

Bronwen Cohen argues in *Caring for Children* that the best strategy for gaining more facilities is a partnership between local authorities and employers. The sorts of initiative being offered by employers desperate to woo women back to work, while being progress of a sort, could disappear just as quickly as they have appeared. Local authorities under the pressure of spending cuts are more likely to be closing nurseries than opening them. However, partnerships can be forged with companies in relation to nurseries and out-of-school provision (how many jobs can cater for a 9–3.30 school day with all the holidays?) which protect the provisions from fluctuations caused by changes in the workforce while relying on investment and funding from employers. There are EC Childcare Network Action Projects being set up in recognition of the fact that Britain has the lowest level of publicly-funded childcare in the EC and also one of the lowest rates of employment in the industrial world for women with children under five.[96]

Now is a good time to fight for these services, which should be seen as a right not a privilege. Employers are more likely to be responsive as they realise that without good standard childcare, women are unable to return to their jobs or stay at work if the childcare they are using breaks down or is not good for their kids. If you can face an employer with the obvious need, backed up by a survey of present staff including those on maternity leave or who have failed to return to work, you may find progress is possible. If you're in a trade union you should find it sympathetic to your campaign and if there is more than one union at work, get together and organise a joint approach. Persistence pays off and you could end up with a generally far better atmosphere at work, one which is more responsive to your needs as a woman worker.

A senior officer at the GLC commented six months after the workplace nursery was set up in premises within County Hall:

It makes a fantastic difference to the feel of the place occasionally sighting toddlers running down the corridors or meeting children in the lifts. Having a successfully run nursery here has done so much to the attitudes towards working women and to work in general, I suppose it's like it's humanised it. All our other worthy and of course important equal opportunities policies feel like they've made only a dent in the overwhelming prejudices against women by comparison.

Checklists

Repetition Strain

1 How would you describe your general health? Excellent, good, average or bad?
2 Do you suffer from swellings, numbness, tingling, 'pins and needles', stiffness, aches or pain in any of the following parts of your body (tick appropriate boxes):

	Swellings	Numbness	Tingling	Stiffness	Aches	Pain
Back						
Neck						
Shoulders						
Arms						
Wrists						
Fingers						
Legs						
Other						

3 Have you visited your doctor about any of these complaints? What diagnosis or treatment did the doctor suggest?
4 Do you have any of the following *types of movement* in your job?
a repetitive movements of the wrists or hands?
b repetitive movements of the arms or shoulders?
c frequent use of awkward wrist positions or bending of the wrists?
d a twisting 'clothes-wringing' motion of the hands and wrists?
e keeping parts of your body in a fixed position, with your muscles tense? (e.g. holding your arms above your shoulders; holding your elbows out)
f repeated stretching or reaching movements?
g repeated squeezing, screwing, pressing or twisting movements?
5 Is your *workstation* well designed for the job you do? For example:
a Can you 'sit square' to do your job?
b Does your chair have good back support?
c Is your chair easily adjustable?
d Is your bench or desk too high or too low?
e Do you have difficulty in reaching the controls, levers etc?
f Do you have repeatedly to stretch or reach in a particular direction to carry out your work?
6 Does the machine/process-line/management, etc, determine the speed of your work, or do you?
7 Is your output measured/is there a monitoring system in operation?
8 What work-rate/piece-rate do you have to achieve?
9 How often do you take a rest break?
10 Can you think of any obvious and immediate improvements that could be made to your job?
11 Have you ever raised any of these problems with your boss/-management?
12 Have any of your workmates complained of painful hands, wrists, arms, shoulders, neck or back?
13 Do you take pain-killers frequently in order to keep working?
14 Are there any other comments you would like to make?

Ventilation

1 Is your office too stuffy?
2 Do people complain of stuffy noses, dry throats, running or itchy eyes, headaches and lethargy?

3 Is your office too draughty?
4 Do people complain of getting 'flu a lot in the office or feeling a lot better when they've been away from the office a while (and getting worse on coming back)?
5 Have the air flow and humidity been checked in your office?
6 Has the air conditioning been checked and serviced on a regular basis?
7 Does your office seem too smoky?

Dangerous Substances

1 Do you use any chemicals or solvents in your office?
2 Have you seen the manufacturers' hazards data sheets for the substances you use?
3 Has your employer carried out, or hired independent consultants to carry out, an assessment of workplace hazards as required under the Control of Substances Hazardous to Health (COSHH) regulations by 1 January 1990?
4 Are there any smells or fumes in your office?
5 Is there any asbestos in your office walls or behind false ceilings, etc?

The Basics

1 Does your office seem too crowded?
2 Does everyone have 40 square feet of space in your office (not including furniture)?
3 Are people happy in your open plan office?
4 Do you have enough toilets? Are they kept clean?
5 Do you have a cloakroom?
6 Is fresh drinking water available?
7 If you have a microwave oven, is it regularly serviced and checked for leakage?
8 Is your office clean?
9 Is your office well decorated?
10 Do you have a first aid box and qualified first aider?
11 Do you have a rest room?
12 Is there any provision made for people with children?
13 Has your employer considered the provision of a workplace nursery and/or subscribing to one?

Notes

1 P. Kinnersly, *The Hazards of Work: How to Fight Them* (London, 1973), p. 49.
2 J. Stellman, *Women's Work, Women's Health: Some Myths and Realities* (New York, 1977), p. 113.
3 G. R. C. Atherley et al., 'Moderate acoustic stimuli: the inter-relation of subjective importance and certain physiological changes', *Ergonomics*, No. 13, 1970, pp. 536–45.
4 T. Nurminen and K. Kurppa, 'Occupational noise exposure and course of pregnancy', *Scandinavian Journal of Work Environment and Health*, No. 15, 1989, pp. 117–24.
5 HSC, *Noise at Work Regulations 1989* (HMSO, October 1989).
6 International Labour Office, *Encyclopaedia of Occupational Health and Safety* (third edition, 1983).
7 A clear explanation can be found in British Society for Social Responsibility in Science, *Noise: Fighting the Most Widespread Industrial Disease* (BSSRS, 1975).
8 A. Hricko, *Working for Your Life* (San Francisco, 1976), p. 8.
9 *Building Research Establishment Digest*, Nos. 128, 129, 153, 163, available from BRF, Garston, Watford, Herts.
10 *The Daily Hazard*, March 1986.
11 *Lighting at Work*, HS/G 38 (HMSO, 1987).
12 C. McGhie, 'Keeping a low profile', *Time Out*, 7–13 September 1979.
13 'Fluorescent lighting, headaches and eye-strain', presented to the National Lighting Conference, 1988.
14 *Fluorescent Lighting: A Health Hazard Overhead* (London Hazards Centre, March 1987).
15 Offices, Shops and Railway Premises Act, Section 8.
16 A. Robertson et al., 'Building sickness, are symptoms related to the office lighting?', *Annual Occupational Hygiene*, Vol. 33, No. 1, 1989, p. 47.
17 *Architects' Journal*, 30 January 1974, p. 236.
18 Illuminating Engineering Society, *IES Code for Interior Lighting* (London, 1973).
19 Alfred Marks Bureau, *Fitness in the Office* (London, 1975).
20 J. Stellman, *Women's Work, Women's Health: Some Myths and Realities* (New York, 1977), p. 103.
21 Personal communication, Women and Work Hazards Group.
22 Offices, Shops and Railway Premises Act, Section 14.

23 Nachemison, cited in E. Grandjean and W. Hunting, 'Ergonomics of posture', in *Applied Ergonomics*, Vol. 8, No. 3, 1977, pp. 135–40.

24 F. M. Troisi, 'Lumbago with spinal disorders caused by incorrect sitting postures during sedentary work', in *Medicina del Lavore*, Vol. 60, No. 1, January 1965, pp. 21–7.

25 Peter Buckle and David Stubbs, 'The contribution of ergonomics to the rehabilitation of back pain patients', *Journal of Social Occupational Medicine*, Vol. 39, 1989, pp. 56–60.

26 British Standards Institution, *Draft British Standard Recommendations for Ergonomics Requirements for Design and Use of Visual Display Terminals in Offices* (BSI, 1987).

27 'Gas-lift chair warning', *IPCS Bulletin 10*, September 1987, p. 5.

28 F. Gilbreth and L. Gilbreth, 'Fatigue study', in *British Standards Institution 3044*, 1958.

29 L. Noro and A. Koskela, 'Some observations on human engineering problems in office work', in *Medical Bulletin*, Vol. 21, No. 2, July 1961, pp. 161–6.

30 S. Laner, *Fitting the Job to the Worker* (Paris, 1963).

31 U. Burandt and E. Grandjean, 'The effect of office seat squabs of various shapes on sitting posture', *Internationale Zeitschrift für Angewandte Physiologue Einschleisslich Arbeitphysiologie*, Vol. 20, No. 5, 1964, pp. 441–52.

32 Personal communication with Marianne Craig.

33 M. Mauriel, 'Static disorders during sedentary work in particular in shorthand typists', in *Archives Maladies Professionelles*, Vol. 27 No. 1, January-February 1966, pp. 74–8.

34 London Hazards Centre, *Repetition Strain Injuries – Hidden Harm from Overuse*, London Hazards Centre Trust Limited, January 1988.

35 Anonymous letter to *Hazards Bulletin*, No. 18, April 1988, p. 11.

36 *Work Hazards*, July 1978, Australia.

37 See the *UK Press Gazette*, 20 February 1989, for a discussion of their negotiations with management for adequate rest breaks and recognition of the disease.

38 *The Journalist*, April 1987, London.

39 *Financial Times*, 6 May 1989 and *BIFU Report*, May 1989.

40 Taken from London Hazards Centre, *Repetition Strain Injuries – Hidden Harm from Overuse*, London Hazards Centre Trust Limited, January 1988.

41 'Many inspectors encountered the increasing problem of main-taining suitable temperatures in modern buildings with large areas of glass. Examples of room temperatures of over 40 degrees C have been recorded in new office blocks, and there have been cases of employees suffering from heat exhaustion.

Excessive heat builds up on sunny days, yet paradoxically the heat lost through the glazing during the night or on dull days can cause difficulties in maintaining a comfortable temperature. Thus the temperature in part of a building exposed to the sun can be intolerable whilst the temperature on the shaded side can be below the required level.

Solar gain in modern buildings is a structural problem and is closely related to the type of building, its ventilation and heating systems, its design and aspect. Architects often underestimate or ignore its effect. Little can be done after the design stage because it is so expensive.

Tinted glass, reflective plastic film, blinds and airconditioning can be utilised to reduce its effect. More research into structural solar shields and structural insulation of modern buildings is needed before there is a really satisfying solution.' (HM Factory Inspectorate, *Report for Offices, Shops and Railway Premises Act for 1972–1973*, HMSO, 1974.

42 'Workers survey the damage', *Daily Hazard*, No. 14, London Hazards Centre, September 1987, p. 4.

43 The Offices, Shops and Railway Premises Act, Section 6, also states that no heating system must be used which 'results in the escape into the air . . . of any fumes of such a character and of such an extent as to be injurious or offensive to persons working [on the premises].'

44 HM Inspectorate, *Annual Report for Offices, Shops and Railway Premises Act for 1970* (HMSO, 1971).

45 'Summertime: the heat's on workers' *Daily Hazard*, No. 13, London Hazards Centre, July 1987, p. 2.

46 Harris street survey of 1135 men and women conducted by Harris for Nisses Millbank Ltd and Moss and Partners Chartered Surveyors. Reported in *Environmental Health News*, 7 July 1989, p. 4.

47 *Sick Building Syndrome* (Labour Research Department) August 1989.

48 See The Heating and Ventilation Contractors' Association Guide, *How to Avoid Sick Building Syndrome*, which contains checklists on office planning, designing air conditioning, fault

finding in air conditioning and a simple questionnaire. Available from: 34 Palace Court, London W2 4JG.

49 *London Hazards Centre*, 'Workers survey the damage', *Daily Hazard*, No. 14, September 1987, p. 4.

50 *Hazards Bulletin*, No. 13, April 1987, p. 2.

51 'Sick building syndrome – a review', special inspector's report no. 10, Health and Safety Executive, June 1988.

52 In S. Wilson and A. Hedge, *The Office Environment Survey: A Study of Building Sickness*, Building Use Studies, 1984, 4373 workers were questioned in 46 buildings across the country. Eighty per cent of the sample experienced symptoms of ill health. Generally, older buildings, public sector ones and ones with water-based air conditioning systems were the worst offenders. An interesting suggestion that the researchers put forward is that tolerable thresholds are reduced in many air-conditioned buildings 'because the occupants are less able to exert personal control over conditions' (p. 4). They also link building sickness to the fact that air conditioning blocks out a sense of the outside. They conclude: 'The causes of building sickness syndrome may be neither mysterious nor sinister, but lie with the fact that in many buildings complex services are required which no one is prepared to pay for.'

53 Offices, Shops and Railway Premises Act 1963, Section 7.

54 International Labour Office, *Hygiene in Shops and Offices*, 1963, p. 34.

55 *TUC Health and Safety at Work 7*, A Course for Union Representatives (TUC Education, 1979).

56 Health and Safety Executive, *Occupational Exposure Limits 1990* (HMSO, January 1990).

57 'Chloroethanes: review of toxicity', in *Current Intelligence Bulletin*, 21 August 1978.

58 See *HSE Guidance Note EH22*, 'Ventilation of buildings: fresh air requirements', 1979.

59 Ralph Nader, *Bitter Wages: Study Group Report on Disease and Injury on the Job* (New York, 1973), p. 34.

60 BSSRS, *Asbestos – Killer Dust*, 1979.

61 Health and Safety Executive, *Work with Man-made Mineral Fibres*, HSE Press Release, 24 June 1989.

62 'Mineral fibre board agreement at BT', *Health and Safety Information Bulletin 137*, 5 May 1987, pp. 9–10.

63 See 'From dust to dust – a safety rep's guide to the hazards of dust at work', TUC leaflet, May 1984 or 'TUC handbook on

dust at work', 1984, for guidance on how to convince fellow workers and management of the need to tackle dust problems.

64 London Hazards Centre inquiry case records, London Hazards Centre Trust, 1989.

65 *Hazards Bulletin*, No. 1, September 1984, p. 7.

66 Fiona McNally, *Women for Hire: A Study of the Female Office Worker* (London, 1979), p. 161.

67 H. P. Cemach, *Work Study in the Office* (Surrey, 1958).

68 OSRPA, Section 5 (2).

69 HMFI (Her Majesty's Factory Inspectorate, replaced by Health and Safety Executive, HSE), 'Report on the Application of the Offices, Shops and Railway Premises Act for 1967'.

70 City Centre, 'VDU work and stress survey', *Safer Office Bulletin*, March 1989.

71 Rosemary Pringle, *Gender at Work* (London, 1986).

72 See *Passive Smoking at Work*, Health Education Authority, 1988, and *Smoking Policies at Work*, Health Education Authority, 1988. The US Surgeon General issued the first ever estimate of deaths in the US caused by passive smoking: c. 3500 p.a. By analogy the figure in Britain would be c. 750 p.a. (data from Radio 4, *Today* programme, 11 May 1990; US memorandum of 10 May 1990).

73 *Municipal and Public Service Journal*, 28 January 1966, p. 272.

74 Personal communication with Marianne Craig in 1978.

75 OSRPA, Section 9.

76 OSRPA, Section 10.

77 OSRPA, Section 57.

78 OSRPA, Section 15.

79 London Hazards Centre, *Southwark Health and Safety at Work Kit*, Action Sheet 3, 1987.

80 GMB, 'Microwave ovens', *Hazards in the Health Service* (GMB, 1984), p. 54. See also GMB, *Risks à la Carte* (GMB, 1986) p. 26.

81 OSRPA, Section 4.

82 London Hazards Centre, 'Insect infestations factsheet – 1', *Daily Hazard*, No. 22, June 1989, p. 3.

83 London Hazards Centre, 'Insect infestations factsheet – 2', *Daily Hazard*, No. 23, September 1989, p. 3.

84 OSRPA, Section 4.

85 International Labour Office, *Encyclopedia of Occupational Safety and Health* (Geneva, 1972), p. 929.

86 *A Much Needed Measure: The Offices Regulation Bill*.

87 Reg. 3 (4) (12), No. 62, 1987, pp. 12–14.

88 'Survey on first aid regulations' (internal report), in *Health and Safety Commission Newsletter 53*, June 1987.

89 The GMB have guidelines on numbers of first aiders:

Number of employees	Number of first aiders
<150	6
150–300	9–12
>300	12–15

GMB, *First Aid at Work*.

90 M. Phil. CNAA 1984, Eileen Phillips, 'Gender and skill – the reconstruction of clerical work with new technology'.

91 Reported in *Labour Research*, December 1987.

92 Maggie Meade-King, 'Hard nursery times ahead', *The Guardian*, 25 April 1989, p. 44.

93 Report for the European Commission's Childcare Network, 1988.

94 *Workplace Nurseries Negotiating Pack*, Workplace Nurseries Campaign, 1988.

95 Childcare Now, Wesley House, 4 Wild Court, London WC2B 5AU.

96 For more information, contact: Bronwen Cohen, UK Expert Representative, EC Childcare Network, c/o Equal Opportunities Commission, Overseas House, Quay Street, Manchester M3 3HN.

3
Physical Hazards

Injury

Every year, 5000 office workers receive injuries which make them absent from work for more than three days. Contrary to the message on most safety posters, injuries at work are rarely caused by individual carelessness or by 'accident-prone' workers. The real causes are poorly designed jobs, pressure of work and bad maintenance of equipment and fittings, so most 'accidents' are preventable. In 1987–8 250 workers received 'fatal or major' injuries in office accidents.[1] This hardly conjures up the commonly accepted picture of offices as safe, clean, trouble-free places to work in.

Many factors contribute to the cause of an accident: temperature, humidity, noise, fatigue, monotony, time of day, stress, production pressures, poor equipment, lack of staff, inadequate funds spent on safety precautions. The cascade of safety magazines put out by ROSPA and the British Safety Council (for example) flooding the market, are mainly for managers and safety officers and a vehicle for advertising protective clothing. As VDUs are more and more in use in offices, there is some useful advice being put forward about workplace design and the precautions which should be taken to prevent damage to office workers' health. But it is still more likely that these magazines will advertise 'radiation pinnies' to protect workers, rather than advocate proper breaks from the screen and the monitoring of office staff's health and fitness.

The main emphasis of most safety propaganda is that accidents are caused by careless workers. These firms (who are so concerned about your safety) say little about how to file a claim for compensation. There is hardly a word either about stress or toxic hazards in the workplace. Putting the burden of safety on to the individual saves a company money.

The 5000 injuries sustained by office workers in Britain each year are only the *reported* accidents. The level is probably nearer 20,000. A study by the National Institute of Industrial Psychology showed that in companies with medical centres, between 55 and 70 per cent of observed accidents were reported; where no medical centre existed, the accidents that were reported were as low as 5 per cent.[2]

Trips and Falls

Almost half the injuries in offices are caused by trips and falls. Check the following in your office:

- Are floors, steps, passages and gangways soundly constructed and well maintained? Are they kept free from obstruction and slippery surfaces? Some manufacturers claim their floor coverings are non-slip when they're not. Special anti-slip material should be used at lift and building entrances.
- Do all staircases have a substantial handrail on any open side? Iron steps to a boiler house in a new office block were railed on one side only, and a worker was seriously hurt when he fell off the unrailed side. An inspector visiting a London cinema found unlocked doors opening on to cavities with drops of 4 feet 6 inches.
- Are files and stationery stacked out of reach? Do you have to risk breaking a leg to reach equipment you need? You can get step stools that lock into place, with spring-mounted retractable castors, and a rubber mat on the stepping surface.
- Are telephone leads and other cables and wires near walls battened down, over seven feet up out of the way, or laid under foot? Ramps can reduce the risk of tripping. If there is a 'spaghetti junction' of wires, there are not enough power points. Jenny Malcolm received a permanent back injury from tripping over a telephone wire in her office. Twenty years later it is still causing her enough problems to prevent her working.
- Are all accesses, staircases and stores well lit? In 1986, the High Court found that an employee who was injured when he stumbled while walking down a flight of stairs, parts of which were unlit, was entitled to damages for his injury on the grounds that the employer had failed in its duty to provide 'sufficient and suitable lighting'.[3]
- Are company car-parks and pavements around the office building kept clear and safe?

Lifting

The second most common cause of injury is strain from over-exertion. Office machines, supplies, file drawers and furniture often need to be moved. If you have to lift something, don't risk your back – ask someone to help you. Remember, there is often no cure for back strain. If equipment needs to be lifted regularly, then demand more staff. In the civil service and in some companies porters are specifically employed to transport supplies.

By law, you have a right to refuse to lift or carry anything very heavy. Section 23(1) of OSRPA states: 'no person shall in the course of his work . . . be required to lift, carry or move a load so heavy as to be likely to cause injury to him [sic]'.

You are also protected by section 7 of the Health and Safety at Work Act:

It shall be the duty of every employee while at work to take reasonable care for the health and safety of himself and of other persons who may be affected by his acts or omissions at work.

This is a favourite section of the Health and Safety at Work Act used by employers to discipline workers and quoted at the top of their safety policy. Now you can quote it back. You could argue that you'd be breaking the law by carrying something heavy enough to injure you. There is no relevant legal maximum weight that office workers may carry, so it's best to use these sections to refuse to carry weights *you* believe are too heavy.

However, current provisions prohibit the employment of any person to lift, carry or move a load so heavy as to be likely to cause injury. A recent European Commission proposal for a Council Directive on manual handling of heavy loads required employers: 'to prevent, as far as possible, the handling of heavy loads without mechanical assistance.'[4] The Health and Safety Commission has also published proposals on handling loads at work. Unfortunately, it has withdrawn its original proposals for 'action levels' based on specific weight ranges – but the new proposals do require employers to make, and keep up to date, an assessment of the handling operations to ensure compliance with Regulation 4 which states: 'Every employer shall take all necessary steps to prevent reasonably foreseeable injury to his employees from the handling of loads at work by those employees.'[5]

In the civil service only weights 'within each person's capacity up to a maximum of 35 lb should be lifted, otherwise help should be called for'.[6] There is often no reason why a load should be heavy. You can negotiate with your suppliers to pack goods in smaller quantities.

Shelving and stacking areas should be arranged to reduce lifting height and carrying distances. Trolleys should be on hand for easy moving of equipment, and felt pads under typewriters mean they can be pushed short distances.

Employers and safety officers like to blame workers for not lifting 'properly'. Well, you can probably ignore all the propaganda about 'proper lifting techniques'. According to the *American Industrial Hygiene Association Journal*, 'In spite of enthusiastic promotion of lifting training – "straight back, bent knees" – the percentage of back injuries in the working population has not materially decreased over the last forty years.'[7] And the International Labour Office says that there is no published evidence that lifting instructions reduce back injury. The danger of employers emphasising lifting techniques is that they are covered if there's an accident, and you are not. The burden should be on *management* to make the workplace safe and healthy.

Machinery and Mechanical Hazards

There's hardly an office in the country without machinery. Automation, and therefore danger, is increasing (see chapters 2 and 4).

- An office worker leant over an addressing machine and her hair became entangled in a roller spindle. She received a bruised temple and jaw.
- An experienced operator suffered amputation of a finger when he opened the side panel in a drawing office printing machine after he'd started it up.
- A man had his finger bones crushed by a stapler and was absent from work for six weeks.
- A woman was cleaning the cylinder of the office multilith printing machine, which was was not switched off at power. The rotating cylinder caught her bracelet and pulled her thumb under the cover guard, breaking it.

Guarding

OSRPA[8] (6) requires the fencing off of hazardous office machinery. Photo-electric guards (using a curtain of light beams) make the machinery shut down if a hand moves across the light, and transparent guards, e.g. on a multilith offset duplicator, let you see the work safely. Ideally, all machines should be designed so that they can't operate without the guards in place, but too often safety features are advertised as 'optional extras', and if left off allow faster output while the supervisors turn a blind eye. Some jobs have been speeded up so much that, under pressure, people remove the guards to work faster. Like productivity deals, pressure to work fast is an insidious cause of injury and death in all kinds of work.

Where there is a roller, a fixed guard should be placed in front of it, and it is advisable for the upper roller to be spring-loaded so that it rises if fingers are put into the gap. Machines with a larger gap between the rollers may seem safe, but if a ringed finger gets caught it will be injured.

The table below shows the dangers of office machinery.

Office machinery and its safety hazards

Photocopiers/addressing machines/electrostencil cutters/ duplicators/paper shredders/ inking rollers/rota printing machinery/postal franking machines	can trap and damage fingers, trap and entangle hair
Guillotines	can slice flesh
Hand presses/stitches/paper drills	can damage fingers
Staplers	can crush bones, lacerate fingers
Electronically moving shelving	can trap and squash a whole person
Lifts	can trap limbs; especially hazardous for elderly and disabled workers
Jogger machines	vibrations can cause 'dead finger'

Where the machine is powerdriven it also presents a fire hazard and risk of shocks.

A woman working in the students' union office at a London polytechnic used a jogger machine for five years. The machine vibrated a great deal; so did the operator and the floor. There were no instructions and no proper base for the machine. The woman's fingers and toes developed a numbness that interfered with her daily use of her hands and feet. The doctor diagnosed the condition as 'white finger' (Raynaud's syndrome) caused by the jogger machine.

Faulty siting and/or congestion of machinery will increase hazards by impeding the operator's movement and make inspection and maintenance difficult. Machines should not be placed near the edges of desks or tables. They should have slip-proof pads or anchoring.

Section 17(3) of OSRPA forbids those under the age of 18 to clean moving parts of machinery. But should *anyone* perform such a task if there is risk of injury?

According to section 19, no one may operate a paper cutter or guillotine unless they are trained or supervised.

All office machinery should be regularly serviced to ensure safe operation. Any new machinery or equipment should be red-tagged for danger until all operators know how to operate it safely.

Safety representatives should vet new machinery before it is put in operation. If a sales rep is on the scene, get her or him to test for mechanical and electrical hazards. If they or your boss insist that the equipment is safe, you could request that they prove it by putting their fingers in between the rollers.

Electrical Hazards

Hazards from electrical equipment include shock, fire and certain risks to the eyes and lungs from ozone and radiation. Faulty electrical equipment can electrocute you. Get management to watch out for the following: loose connections, unearthed equipment, damaged cables, defective insulation, overloaded circuits, broken switches, worn or damaged appliances, trailing leads.

Many machines give no indication whatsoever, e.g. by light or noise, that they are switched on. They could be left on all weekend. This 'stresses' the electrical equipment and makes it more hazardous. All equipment should have a clearly marked mains switch. Where several different types of machines are brought together, such as an addressing machine and guillotine attached to a stapler, each from a different manufacturer, there will be a shock hazard because each machine will have a small amount of leakage current, all of which adds up.

The fuse is probably the most abused part of any electrical circuit. Fused plugs designed for a specified type of mains wiring known as the 'ring main' are commonly known as 13 amp plugs. But if a machine only consumes 3 amps of power, then the fuse in the plug should also be 3 amp. Otherwise, if the electrics fail a fire may break out before the fuse blows.

Although normally safe, ordinary mains voltage of 240 volts, such as that supplying office lighting and most simple machines, can cause dangerous currents. There are 38 reported electrical accidents in offices in an average year and these are often caused by not switching off machines. Electric fires can get knocked over and are dangerous if used for drying wet clothes; safe drying facilities should be provided.

Some electrical equipment contains liquids (for example, some photocopiers) which may be spilled over the electrical components. The resultant corrosion can lead to electrical failure. If the liquid conducts electricity, there is a danger of shock to the user via the wet machine and possibly wet hands. Some machines use flammable liquids (for example, spirit duplicators). If these are spilled on an unshrouded electrical switch they can ignite, or the vapour can cause small explosions in the body of the machine. In some electrical machinery you can put your hand into the electric works (for example, some ventilation fans). If you touch a mains voltage, say with a paper clip, it could kill you. And some machinery gets overheated – it's a bad design if it gets too hot to touch or if you can touch the heating elements. Some is a fire risk.

The covers of dangerous areas should not be removable with the machine on; alternatively, the machine should switch off automatically if they are removed. Some photocopiers have this system. Badly designed equipment should be put right or replaced; or it should remain unused by the office staff – although this might shock the boss! All machines should have automatic power cut-outs. This means they should have control and interlock circuits which shut them down at the first indication of trouble or interference. Only qualified electricians should check and maintain electrical machinery.

Static Electricity

Static is generated by a number of things: nylon carpets and upholstery, vinyl floors, formica desk tops, plastic chairs, synthetic clothing. Metal furniture aggravates the problem and you can get nasty (but non-fatal) shocks from touching filing cabinets and switchboards. Electrostatic photocopiers also generate static electricity. Static can be painful on contact and can cause heaviness and pains in the legs. It can be stressful and is especially dangerous if you have a heart condition. There is some evidence that static has an effect on the nervous system of laboratory animals.[9] It may create a fire and explosion risk if it occurs in areas where solvents are stored.

Possible Solutions

Furniture can have earthed conductive mats and plates over non-conductive surfaces. This avoids the build-up of static charge.

Increased humidity reduces the risk of static, which is why some office workers take recourse to watering the carpet. Humidifiers can be installed, but there are health hazards associated with them. Humidifier fever is a 'flu-like illness with symptoms of fever, chills, cough, general malaise, chest tightness and laboured breathing which is caused by breathing in 'organic dust' circulated in the office air by poorly maintained humidifying and air conditioning systems. Indoor plants properly watered will increase humidity and improve the atmosphere.

Earthing wires can be inserted into carpets, or metal or carbon-coated fibres can be incorporated. Carpets may be treated with anti-static agents to increase their conductivity, but this is only a temporary measure. You could demand the installation of carpets with special guarantees against static shock. These are always found in computer rooms, where floor coverings must be anti-static – to protect the *computer*'s 'health'.

Wearing cotton clothing helps. There's no good reason why you should have to change your clothes (it's better to change the office carpet!) but you should have the *right* to do so. In some offices it's compulsory for women to wear skirts and nylon tights – a basic infringement of your rights and your health needs.

Injury from Fittings and Furniture

Crowded offices lead to injuries. You can trip over open bottom file drawers, or fracture your nose or bang your head against open top drawers. If you lean back on a chair on castors it may overturn and you could fracture your skull. One safety rep in the civil service broke her nose on the corner of a free-standing screen. She was absent from work for several weeks and ever since has been plagued with recurrent sinus trouble. Sharp corners, drawers that stick, swing doors, knobs are all dangerous and can be modified to make them safer. Filing cabinets are particularly risky. A CPSA member in the Midlands was crushed by one. File drawers should not open into aisles, and they don't have to be located behind doors! Cabinets should be bolted together, and to the wall, so they *cannot* fall over. A piece of hardwood or strip metal about half an inch thick can be inserted under the front end of a cabinet to improve stability. There should be a fail-safe catch at the back of each drawer to prevent its coming right out and dropping on your foot. The filing of papers in a tightly packed drawer causes cut fingers. More filing space would prevent this.

After the Event

If someone is injured in your department make sure she gets medical attention and that the incident is recorded in the accident book, with all the details about how, where and when it happened. Do not say or sign anything. This may be used against you later (this goes for both safety reps and victims). The only person to whom you must give a signed statement is a health and safety inspector. Make sure you're involved when the employer is filling in accident report forms. Always enter 'near-misses' as well as injuries.

The accident book should be readily accessible to everyone. It is useful to analyse it and to use the information and statistics to argue for prevention of further injuries. Is everyone, including the people who clean your office, aware of where the accident book is kept?

Safety reps should always get to the scene of an accident quickly to record what happened. This could be crucial later if the injured person claims compensation. D. A. Castle, a solicitor, warns management that union safety representatives are liable to be quick on the scene:

The line manager, if properly trained, should get all the witnesses to an accident together immediately and take statements from them. He should then fill in the accident report form. This is the ideal situation: in reality things happen differently. It is more likely that safety representatives, being workmates, will be on the scene quickly and begin asking questions first. Employers who answer these questions may well make admissions in the emotion of the moment which they would otherwise never have made. A safety representative looking for evidence of what occurred would have an admission to report to the solicitors representing the prospective claimant. The employer's insurance company would start with an immediate handicap . . . *the problems really begin* when safety representatives ask to see accident reports and seek to interview employees who witness the accident.[10]

It's bad enough having an accident, without being up against this kind of thinking!

This approach to safety results from the conflict of interest between safety and profit. How many windows are locked and fire escapes blocked for security purposes, to protect the property rather than the employees? How many employers are willing to spend money on an efficient ventilation system or a safe photocopier when you demonstrate that these represent a hazard to health?

A Factory Inspectorate report on the working of OSRPA analysed thirty-five fatal accidents in premises covered by the Act to see how far each accident could have been prevented, and by whom. They concluded:

Number of fatal accidents	Accidents that could have been prevented by
8	management
6	deceased
1	fellow workers
3	deceased and fellow workers together
3	management and deceased together
14	unforeseen circumstances
—	
35	

They say: 'Most of the failures of the management were related to the supply of proper maintenance of equipment, or its inspection and control.'[11] A large proportion of workplace accidents can be put down to *bad management*.

Trade union organisation is the best way of approaching safety. The election of safety reps who carry out regular inspections and lean on management to fulfil their legal duties will do more for health and safety at work than all the commercialised safety propaganda in the land. Get a good safety agreement. Safety reps have the right to vet new machinery. Training is important, since new workers have more accidents than experienced workers. However, the point of training is not to learn how to avoid the danger; it is to *eliminate* the dangers. There should also be training in fire prevention and in first aid, and safety reps must be involved in all training programmes.

Fire

Fire is one of the biggest causes of death and severe injury at work. Much of the material and equipment used in offices is combustible and much of it a very dangerous fire hazard. Here are some examples:

- Cleaning materials and solvents
- Paper and paper dust
- Electrical and mechanical equipment, especially if badly maintained and unguarded
- Gas appliances
- Furnishings
- Insulation materials
- Wax on floors, especially with underfloor heating timber frame structures
- Refuse

Machines using paper in large quantities collect a great deal of paper fluff, which gets into inaccessible cavities and acts as blotting paper for flammable liquids. All that's then needed is a spark. A ventilation fan caught fire in one of London's big libraries, and an electrostencil cutter burst into flames in one Edinburgh school office.

Photocopiers may contain infra-red heaters. If the exhaust fans break down heat soon builds up. Once the heater is alight, toners and dispersants may be set alight.

Old timber-frame offices can be a serious fire hazard, but many are safer than modern buildings. Wall-to-wall carpeting, plastic furniture and combustible partitions are all dangerous. Open plan offices permit an instantaneous flash of fire across the ceiling if the soundproofing is made of combustible material. Some plastics and other synthetics, if set alight, give off fumes which can kill instantly.

Burning carpet backing and underlays emit huge quantities of smoke. A fire at Manchester's Woolworth's which started in the furniture department killed ten people, mainly as a result of fumes from burning polyurethene foam. The *Wall Street Journal*, on 21 January 1981, ran a story about fears for office workers' safety in high-rise office blocks: 'Safety officials fear skyscraper holocaust could kill thousands. They cite buildings' design and location, lax codes, poison gas from plastics.'

A letter from a doctor, J. Stellman, to the *New York Times* on 12 December 1980, argued that fire risks had increased drastically: 'The completely undivided ceiling and floor-to-ceiling windows typical of large open-space offices make it possible for an instantaneous flash of fire to spread.' Modern high-rises are 'criss-crossed with wiring that may become overloaded.' The other terrifying danger is the generation of fumes from burning plastic. Many fire deaths attributed to smoke inhalation, wrote Dr Stellman, 'are more accurately described as due to chemical-fume poisoning'.

Paraffin, acetone and ammonia are highly dangerous – and may be stored in your office. The vapours from most flammable liquids are heavier than air and can be carried by ventilation to other areas where a source of ignition may be present. And it's not only chemicals. As Janet Ross, a clerical worker in a small office, said: 'We are all very afraid of fire, since hundreds of files are not in metal cabinets but in open bookshelves along the room.'

Fire Certificates

If more than twenty people are employed (or more than ten work anywhere other than on ground level), your employer must apply for a fire certificate. This lays down legal requirements for fire precautions in your workplace: means of escape, particulars of highly flammable materials, and so on. Safety reps can inspect and take copies of the fire certificate as part of their rights to information. You can use the certificate to make up a checklist for inspection to help you monitor whether it is being correctly applied by management. Note that they must report any changes (for example, of exits, or in the use of inflammables) to the fire authority, who issues the certificate. Fire precautions in Crown premises are dealt with by HM Inspectorate of Fire Services. In 1989 a new Code of Practice was issued for fire precaution in small workplaces not required to have a fire certificate. The Code provides guidance on the requirements of the *Fire Precautions Act 1971* for 'low risk' premises on the provision and maintenance of means of escape and fire-fighting equipment.[12]

Fire Precautions and Disabled Staff

Special consideration must be given to the needs of disabled staff in fires. The following need to be considered:

1 Identification of everyone who may need special help to get out.
2 Allocation of responsibility to specific able-bodied staff to help disabled staff in emergency situations.
3 Consideration of the best escape routes for disabled staff.
4 Developing procedures to enable lifts to be used where possible (e.g. to identify unaffected lifts, to prevent power loss to lifts being used to evacuate the disabled).
5 Procedures for disabled staff to summon assistance in emergencies.

The problems they raise are not great and management should not refuse to employ disabled staff because of problems in emergencies. They should be pressed to tackle other barriers to the employment of disabled people such as access and toilet facilities[13]

Appliances that become hot should be modified and in the meantime sited away from combustible materials. The flammability factor of carpeting, plastic components and sound proofing should be investigated before they're installed; furnishings can have flame-proof treatment. Flammable liquids should never be used in a confined space. There are special requirements for storing flammable materials. These will be laid down in the fire certificate and in the Highly Flammable Liquids and Liquefied Petroleum Gases Regulations 1972. These lay down the types of containers and storerooms required for various quantities of highly flammable liquid.

Safer substitutes should be used where possible. Check the safety certificates of all fire appliances and machinery. Containers for disposal of scrap and waste and their locations should be safe and designed to prevent fire. Fire doors and automatic sprinklers should be installed where necessary.

Prevention of Fire and Fire Extinguishers

Managements in most places where people work are legally obliged to provide suitable fire-fighting equipment on their premises and to see that it is properly maintained. Portable fire extinguishers are generally the equipment provided, backed up by hose reels and fire buckets.[14]

For general protection water or multi-purpose dry powder extinguishers can be used, but as water is a conductor of electricity it must not be used on live electrical equipment. Halon fire extinguishers are increasingly selected for use in rooms containing electronic equipment because they are less likely than other types to damage sensitive equipment. However, when Halon extinguishers are used toxic products may be produced. Halon vapour on its own is also toxic.

A safer alternative (for the workers) for rooms with electronic equipment would be automatic local carbon dioxide flooding systems with smoke and heat detectors as early warning systems. IPCS safety representatives approached the London Hazards Centre in 1987 when management planned to replace all the carbon dioxide extinguishers with Halon extinguishers which they said were 'cheaper and better'. When the safety reps showed management information from the Hazards Centre detailing the hazards of Halon they offered 'reassurance' that there was little risk as the Halon extinguishers would only be used on little fires and in big fires the workers would evacuate the building anyway![15]

The fire safety department of the local fire brigade will offer advice by phone if necessary. They're usually happy to give lectures and demonstrations. Training in the use of fire-fighting equipment is usually given at the fire station and the employer charged for the service. Note that no one should tackle a fire if it puts them at risk.

The fire service, like the health and safety inspector, has the right to enter premises and inspect the fire precautions. They will investigate complaints, including anonymous ones. If you

Dear *Hazards Bulletin*,

A young girl who sometimes does temp work for our office burst in and threw lighter fuel over a newspaper, set light to it and rapidly puffed it out with a fire extinguisher (which she was carrying around in a briefcase).

She had answered an ad in the *Evening Standard* for salespersons. When she went along initially to the office that produced the fire extinguishers, she had to sign a form saying she realised the fire extinguisher was not recommended by the Fire Offices' Committee (i.e. the insurance companies). She also asked if the contents were safe and the man demonstrated that they were by drinking the stuff.

Anyway back at the Central London Poly, we were all very impressed (though not with the price – £28) and were thinking of placing orders right, left and centre. I looked at the fire extinguisher label and noticed it said 'Contains TCF and SGM'. Pat Kinnersly's book has about half a page on the toxicity of TCF and related substances. Amy, our temp, has now handed in her fire extinguisher. She was advised to ring the HSE Occupational Safety and Hygiene Laboratories at Cricklewood for more gen on TCF and SGM. She was put through to a Dr somebody who said words to the effect that if the company said it was a safe product she should take their word for it and if everybody acted like her then how would any work get done! She was very upset by this response.

Best wishes
Netta Swallow
Central London Poly, 309 Regent Street, London W1

are a safety representative you could send the fire safety officers a list of safety reps from your place of work and ask them to contact the reps about inspection of the offices. It's also worth contacting the firefighters through the local Fire Brigades Union if you need more information.

Escape

Workers in Cheshire County Council's Warrington offices were working in a potential fire trap, built in 1974. One NALGO safety rep had this to say:

This means there are 40 people on each of four floors with literally no escape from their workplace. If the central staircase – the only present escape – is blocked, 160 people could die. I think this is outrageous. Local government is supposed to be a good employer, working in the interests of local people. Yet here they are letting us, their own employees, work in a time bomb! They *knew* it was unsafe! It didn't even fit the regulations when they moved into the building. The reality of the cutbacks is that every day people's lives are put at risk. . . . It's not a natural risk, it's deliberate cutbacks. We're not going to let this issue go.[16]

If there's a fire, what you'll want above all is an easy escape route. Yet many fire escapes are locked or blocked with stores or refuse. In one insurance office in Colchester, the fire escape was blocked because it was next to a loading bay. Make sure you can't be trapped in your office in the event of fire.

Escape routes must be clearly indicated, and particular attention should be given to escape routes from basements and windowless rooms. In computer rooms there should be easy escape, since in the event of fire, the fail-safe systems which protect the computers often flood the place with carbon dioxide or Halon, both of which are toxic gases.

There should be full-scale fire drills at least every six months, so that workers are familiar with escape routes. In one DSS office in the London area there were no fire drills until a safety rep was elected. Management simply said it was unnecessary! APEX carried out a survey of their members' offices and found 68 per cent lacked proper fire drills.

Ursula Huws worked for the Schools Council in London, and there had been no fire practice for two years: 'The branch pressed for fire drills, but we got nowhere. So then we said we'd organise our own fire practice. The threat was enough, and management organised regular ones after that and unblocked the fire doors.'[17]

Automatic systems are now available that can detect heat, smoke or flames and raise the alarm. Alarms must be audible or visible everywhere. Some soundproofing prevents inefficient alarm bells being heard. For example, can the bell be heard in the typing pool and in the lavatories? The bell should be tested or examined every three months at least. Make sure alarms are well maintained – often the hammer is missing.

If you are dissatisfied with anything concerning fire precautions, it should be a matter of negotiation or dispute. Fire precautions are only adequate if *you* think they are.

Checklists

Injury

1 Are accidents and injuries, however small, recorded in your accident book?
2 Are there trailing leads, loose or damaged carpet/tiles or slippery floors in your office?
3 Do your stairs have a good handrail?
4 Are all stairs and walkways well lit?
5 Are all filing cabinets stable and safe?
6 Are all items stored within easy reach?
7 Do you have to lift heavy or awkward objects?
8 Have you been trained to operate office machinery safely?
9 Are all office machines safely guarded?
10 Do you have all electrical equipment and leads serviced on a regular basis?
11 Is faulty electrical equipment reported and taken out of service or labelled?
12 Do you suffer from static in your office?
13 Is all your office furniture safe and in good condition?
14 Are all accidents and near-misses recorded and investigated?
15 Do your trade union safety reps (if you are lucky enough to have them) regularly inspect your office?

Fire

1 Do you know where your nearest fire exit is?
2 Do you have a fire drill at least twice a year?
3 Are your fire alarms checked on a regular basis?
4 Do you know where your nearest fire extinguisher is? How to use it? And what types of fire it can be used on?
5 Does your office need a fire certificate? Have you seen it?
6 If you have staff or visitors with disabilities what arrangements are made for them?
7 Are all materials and substances likely to start a fire stored safely?

Notes

1 'Accident figures for offices and shops', *Health and Safety at Work*, December 1989, p. 23.

2 Workers Educational Association, London District, teaching material, 1978.

3 Reported in *Health and Safety Information Bulletin*, 4 November 1986, p. 15.

4 Proposal for a Council Directive of the minimum health and safety requirements for handling heavy loads where there is a risk of back injury for workers, *Official Journal of the European Communities*, No. C117/8, 4 May 1988.

5 Health and Safety Commission, *Handling Loads at Work – Proposals for Regulations and Guidance* (HSC, 1988).

6 TUC checklist for civil service trade union representatives, fe. LAO Code, paragraph 14.

7 J. R. Brown, 'Factors contributing to the development of low backpain in industrial workers', *American Industrial Hygiene Association Journal*, January 1975, pp. 26–31.

8 OSRPA, Section 17 (1).

9 TUSIU, *A Workers' Guide to Office Hazards* (North-East Trade Union Studies Information Unit, Newcastle, 1979), p. 6.

10 *New Law Journal*, 28 September 1978; emphasis added.

11 *HM Factory Inspectorate Annual Report for 1971* (HMSO, 1972).

12 *Code of Practice for Fire Precautions in Factories, Offices, Shops and Railway Premises not Required to Have a Fire Certificate* (HMSO, 1989).

13 From TUC Education Department, *Health and Safety at Work*, No. 5.

14 Fire Protection Association, *Fire Protection Equipment – Portable Fire Extinguishers*, FE4 (FPA, 1984). Extinguishers should comply with British Standard BS 5423: *Specification for Portable Fire Extinguishers*, and should also be approved by the Fire Officers Committee.

15 London Hazards Centre inquiry case notes: Hazards of Halon, 1987.

16 Personal interview by Marianne Craig in 1978.

17 See note 16.

4
New Technology

What VDUs are doing to Office Work and Office Workers

A young businessman strides into his executive suite, flings his briefcase into an armchair and flicks on the VDU screen on the desk. A few rapid taps of his fingers and he has the answer he was looking for. He reaches for the phone.

A woman, eyes red-rimmed and forehead creased with pain, is hunched in front of a flickering screen, her fingers a blur of movement, her head moving rapidly from screen to document and back again. Behind her is a row of women, all similarly occupied.

Are these the image and the reality of the new technology in operation? An advertisement aimed at paper-bound managers to woo them into buying the newest brand of computer, versus the daily grind experienced by thousands of women office workers across the country? A simple yes needs some qualification. The positive image of computer use may be the reality for certain strata of workers – designers, managers, production engineers, senior administrative staff. Similarly, the gulf between the experience of VDUs for clerical workers and for professional staff is related to the organisation of work, rather than the technology itself. In other words, once a VDU or terminal is installed there is no inevitability about an office worker being tied to the machine eight hours a day, performing intensive, repetitive operations.

The very serious health hazards presented by VDUs which will be discussed in this chapter have been and continue to be extensively researched. Yet unfortunately researchers often fail to make a distinction between the technology itself and the use of VDUs. Sometimes this is intentional, a matter of choosing to assess effects which appear measurable, such as the consequence of glare or flickering screens on eyesight rather than the rising stress levels involved in a routinising of tasks to fit in with a computer program. Or it involves an unspoken acceptance of what can and can't be changed in the office, what kinds of health and safety hazards can and can't be prevented. The recurring point, which cannot be over-emphasised, is that the dangers to operators' health are massively increased once continuous, all-day use is expected of them. Preventing this involves tackling questions of control over work, the way it is divided up, expectations of women workers, skill evaluations and career structures.

Experiences communicated to the City Centre for Office Workers included:

Mrs G, Cornwall:
'On average we use ours for at least six hours per day, the range of key depressions per hour are 17,000 to 21,000. We feel that maybe this is the cause for our backache, eye-strain and stress.'

Ms R, the Norwich Union Insurance Group:
'I sit at a keyboard for generally 6½ hours a day with half an hour break making a 7-hour working day. We are paid on output which for a start puts pressure on us. I certainly suffer from stiff shoulders and aching eyes and I've had time off from work with sciatica.'

Ms C, Bristol:
'I myself for the past six months have been in considerable pain in my neck and shoulders. I have injections and X-rays which do not show anything. I have been a VDU operator for seven years but the last year I have been put in an office 14' by 11' 6" by 8' high with three computers which are being used continuously for 8 hours a day with no break. We are finding that the static is very bad in the office and we are continually receiving shocks from cabinets and even each other.'

These are all issues which employers are far more reluctant to negotiate on than, say, types of office furniture or placing of VDU screens. Their resistance stems from what they see as attempts to encroach on their right to manage. Or in some cases they cling to the status quo because even if it has disadvantages, at least it's not unknown territory. Trade unions as workers' organisations are not entirely free of the wish not to rock the boat. However, given their intention to negotiate with management on behalf of workers, they do provide a crucial means of challenging management presuppositions about what constitutes an acceptable job or bearable conditions of work.

Controlling Office Workers

Earlier in the book there was a brief outline of how much office work has changed during this century. The assembly-line in manufacturing industry accelerated the move away from craft workers who had been involved in the whole production process, towards a workforce whose value to an employer was their ability to repeat as quickly as possible simple, unskilled operations. This deskilling has been mirrored in the office, with clerks no longer in a position eventually to step into the manager's shoes. Instead, enormous numbers of office workers carry out repetitive tasks which are only one fragment of the overall information gathering, retrieving and analysing process.

Most management arguments which attempt to justify this organisation of work insist that it brings increases in efficiency and productivity. A less publicised argument is that it ensures greater management control over the workforce. Taking away from workers any decision-making over how, what or when they do something next, saves management from any dependency on the initiative, commitment or knowledge of their employees. It doesn't matter if jobs are boring or mindless because the work can be done whatever the motivation of the worker. Significantly, it also gives grounds for offering low wages – any workers who demand more can, after all, easily be replaced.

Computers are the perfect tool for reinforcing this trend. Or, in the case of the 'old-fashioned' offices which still rely on what staff have inside their heads, for introducing new methods which can replace their skill and expertise. As a VDU operator put it in a survey done by the clerical union, APEX:

> The use of the VDU in a job would be all right if it was used in moderation, say a couple of hours a day, but using one 7½ hours a day, constantly, is just awful. Any part of the job which required some brain work now seems to be prohibited. It seems rather a waste of time to take so-called skilled clerks and turn them into punch operators, which is just about all

we do. There is absolutely no brain work involved in the job. If VDU work could be combined with some other work which required mental exertion, then it wouldn't be so bad.[1]

However, this pessimistic picture of computerisation success-fully drawing out all the skills and knowledge of workers so as to demote them to machine attendants needs to be viewed with a little scepticism. In the United States, where computerisation has been more comprehensively implemented than in Britain, there is some recognition of the inefficiency of 'over-computeris-ation'. For example, General Motors decided in the early eight-ies to hold back on its computerisation programme because it had found that instead of increasing efficiency, it had caused the 'loss' of huge numbers of components through operators receiving computer instructions which they found meaningless.[2] It's a cogent argument that can be put to any management engaged in enthusiastic systems analysis or time and motion studies which aim to drive a wedge between tasks set for employees and their overall understanding of the complete work process. If you ask people to act like dummies, then the chances are they will.

Any managerial strategy that expects to create the job of VDU operator – someone whose sole task is to input data to a computer system – can be confronted with questions about the ultimate inefficiency that will result. Whether feeding in data or receiving instructions on a computer handout, if nothing is known of the significance of any task, the probability of its being hard to rectify mistakes is massively increased. This argument obviously goes hand in hand with the severe risk to employees' health caused by continuous VDU operation, but in some situ-ations may find a more receptive ear in managements who have been 'sold' a new system.

Companies which produce software – the computer programs which enable the hardware (the box) to function – are often keen to appeal to managers by offering them a means of checking on their workers. 'Spying' on how quickly or accurately words are typed, data is input, commands are met, is a different strategy from reorganising work so that no initiative is required (or possible) from the employee. It may have a very immediate attraction to employers. Wang, the manufacturers of word pro-cessors, point out to buyers: 'A built-in reporting system helps you monitor your work flow. It automatically gives the author's

and typist's names, the document number, the date and time of origin and last revision, the required editing time, and the length of the document.' If you suspect that this kind of monitoring system is in place at your work, you can always ring the manufacturer to check, presenting yourself as a potential buyer. It is possible for unions to negotiate to outlaw such practices. The agreement won by AUEW/TASS and TGWU/ACTSS at Ford Motor Company included the following: 'All information acquired specifically or incidentally by computer systems shall not be used for individual or collective work performance measures.'

A carrot which may be held out to VDU operators for accepting an in-built monitoring system is Payment by Results (PBR). Bonus schemes which offer extra payments for increases in keystrokes are a fundamental threat to operators' health. It is rare for employers to offer bonus schemes in jobs predominantly done by women. And it has been accepted that bonuses are a crucial part of the package which continues to keep average rates of pay for men much higher than women's. Despite equal pay legislation women's wages still stand at 73 per cent of men's. For example, a study of local authority employees in London in 1987[3] showed women still consistently earning less than men despite their union (NUPE) having negotiated re-gradings which had pushed women up the hierarchy. Although home helps, for instance (predominantly women), had been negotiated a place in the grading structure above refuse collectors (predominantly men) they were still earning *less* because bonus payments were a much larger element in the jobs where the majority of men worked.

These sorts of finding act as a strong incentive for women to accept productivity schemes in VDU work which could push up their pay. However, the carrot must be resisted. The stress already generated by continuous VDU operating means that any incentive scheme can only cause an unacceptable increase in health risk. It is also likely that the ultimate effect of accepting PBR is to push up the standard rate above which any bonuses are measured.

The following case dealt with by the London Hazards Centre in 1989 shows how workers can end up paying with their health for PBR systems.

Fifty data-entry operators working for the Prudential Assurance in Reading had every moment of their working lives measured and had to average at least 10,000 keystrokes per hour, otherwise they would be moved off the job. They were expected to average over 85 per cent actual keyboarding time – 51 minutes in every hour of a 35-hour working week.

Keystroke rates of 15,000–20,000 per hour were common and some women were hitting up to 27,000. They were locked into a vicious PBR system which awarded just 8p per hour for each extra 500 keystrokes over 10,000.

Not surprisingly, many of the women experienced stress, postural and musculo-skeletal problems, eye-strain and headaches. A new data entry system allowed the manager to monitor keystroke rates and to use the results either to cut wages or jack up productivity by some 20–25 per cent for the same pay. With the ever-present threat of work being put out to agencies, the women were forced to increase their output, with a corresponding increase in health problems.[4]

The TUC recommends that:

no VDU operator should be paid wholly or partly by means of incentive payment schemes based on keystroking or error-free operation. Such schemes encourage excessive workspeeds with greatly increased stress on the workers involved. For the same reasons keyboard speed 'competitions' with prizes should not be permitted.[5]

Ill Effects – Establishing the Damage

These issues of deskilling, controlling and monitoring office staff and intensifying the pace of work are central in any strategies that question management's right to force jobs on people which will make their working lives a misery. The possible ill effects which can result if managers are allowed to get away with it include eye-strain, stress, muscle and body pain, skin rashes and reproductive hazards. A survey by the Labour Research Department (LRD) in 1985 of 7000 VDU screens used by 17,000 workers shows evidence of a wide range of health problems directly linked to VDU operation.[6]

One of the difficulties facing negotiators is that although operators complain of sore eyes, dryness or burning sensations, eye tics and conjunctivitis, employers may still demand evidence of permanent damage to eyesight before agreeing to changes in work practices. The Health and Safety Executive state in their leaflet *Working with VDUs*: 'There have been several studies on whether working with a VDU can affect an operator's eyes. None of them has found any evidence to suggest that VDUs cause damage to the eyes or eyesight or make existing eye defects worse.' Similarly, LRD approached seven eye consultants, all of whom were reluctant to confirm eye damage. 'Comfort . . . should not be confused with health,' said one.

There are two counter-arguments which should be put. First, the lack of evidence proving damage to eyesight does not prove that damage never occurs. As the Association of Optical Practitioners communicated to LRD in July 1985: 'We feel there is a need to monitor workers' eyes for a prolonged period to establish the true position.' Second, eye-strain is often muscular fatigue caused by the muscles having to work for long periods doing the same thing. Research suggests that in the case of both colour distortion and eye fatigue, sight rapidly returns to normal *with rest*. In the absence of rest, deterioration could well occur.

The most accurate assessment of strain and rest requirements must be operators' own experience of discomfort. This makes a strong case for both introducing regular eye tests and rest breaks away from the screen, based on surveying the levels of fatigue felt by operators. Given findings such as the survey done by the civil service union, CPSA, in 1984 of the British Telecom Bristol Computer Centre[7] which showed one in three operators suffering regularly from headaches and 75 per cent suffering from fatigue, there are very strong grounds for responding to the experiences of those who actually use the machines. A number of unions have recommendations and agreements regarding rest breaks (see Appendix I).

The TUC guidelines referred to above set out a number of recommendations in relation to acceptable lighting levels and positioning of screens and avoidable glare. These cover in detail all the ergonomic aspects of VDUs, including, for instance, the conflict between the lighting level suitable for general office work (between 500 and 1000 lux) and that appropriate to VDU use. Some manufacturers recommend levels below 300 lux which would condemn VDU users to work in dimly-lit offices. The TUC recommends a compromise of between 300 and 500 lux as a general lighting level with additional task lights to illuminate source documents.

The recommended maximum daily work time on a VDU in these guidelines is 50 per cent and for rest pauses, breaks of at least 15 minutes every hour when the work is intensive and 15 minutes every two hours otherwise. The TUC recognises the danger in pushing for only half the working day to be available for VDU work. One obvious employer response, particularly given that it is largely women who do this work, is to substitute part-time jobs for full-time ones. This may force negotiators back into a position of insisting on adequate rest breaks, taken away from the screen in a rest area.

A problem which may then arise is that although certain rest breaks have been agreed, there is no certainty that staff will be in a position to take them. A health and safety survey undertaken for the London Borough of Newham and Newham NALGO in September 1986 by North-East London Polytechnic underlined this. The Health and Safety Manual there lays down that VDUs should not be operated by an individual employee for more than 50 minutes without a break – a ruling that nearly all the staff were aware of. But the researchers were told time and again by staff that this wasn't possible, and neither was the 240 minutes per day limit. As one office worker put it:

It's no good having rules and guidelines . . . no matter whether the management turn round and say 'right you can use the VDU for 2, 3 or 4 hours a day', if it's impossible to carry out your job within the guidelines that have been laid down, then people will actually do what they feel they have to do.[8]

One possible solution may be to have the rest breaks programmed in to the computer software itself, or at least to explore ways of using the technology to create conditions that allow workers to take their agreed breaks. It is a dilemma that relates back to the issues raised at the beginning of the chapter about the organisation of work. Avoiding deleterious effects to the health of office staff means creating jobs that don't require tying workers to machines in order to repeat simple and intensive tasks. Unless some control in terms of decision-making and initiative is expected of the employees, then despite a progressive agreement, pressures from supervisers or even the workers themselves, can lead to the demands of the job rather than health and safety considerations prevailing.

The sort of pace of work and relentless nature of VDU operating which causes eye-strain has been shown to have extreme effects on stress levels. Depression, anxiety, irritability, even heart problems such as spasm caused by lack of oxygen to the heart muscle[9] have been linked to VDU work which operators find is demanding too fast a pace of work from them. Establishing what causes what is very difficult when it comes to discussing job dissatisfaction and stress. As anyone knows who dreads going to work on Monday morning, who feels their body tense as they set foot inside the lift taking them up their office, they are likely to find their job stressful and to show signs of it in their health. Equally, if the job is stressful, they are likely to feel trepidation about starting the weekly grind and express themselves as very dissatisfied about work. What is undeniable is that levels of health are inextricably linked to experiences of stress, and managements which are faced with high rates of sickness in their workforces would do well to discover how to reorganise methods and pace of work.

Two other major areas of worry for VDU workers are reproductive hazards and Repetitive Strain Injury (RSI). In both cases the consequences can be tragic if they go undetected for any length of time and they are also both dangers which medical opinion is still reluctant to confirm. For example, the Health and Safety Executive state:

> Higher levels [of miscarriage] have been reported among groups of VDU operators; but investigations show that they are not peculiar to VDU work. The very latest research studies have not been able to show a link between miscarriage or birth defect and VDUs.[10]

Just two years after the HSE dismissed the possibility of a link between VDU work and miscarriage, a major US study found a doubling of miscarriage rates among women who work at VDUs more than 20 hours a week.[11]

In September 1984, an Industrial Tribunal found that a pregnant library assistant's fears over the possible health risks of VDUs were 'by no means ill-founded'. Hazel Johnston was sacked by Inverness Highland Regional Council because she refused to do VDU work for two hours a day. The employers had taken advice from the Employment Medical Advisory Service which is part of the factory inspectorate and concluded there was no risk to the foetus. The Industrial Tribunal found her dismissal unfair and favoured her re-instatement.

What is clear is that there is no irrefutable evidence proving *no* connection between VDU work and miscarriage, birth defects or infertility – the latter obviously being something that directly affects men too. In the light of this the TUC recommend that 'until more conclusive scientific evidence becomes available on the presence or absence of a link between VDU work and reproductive hazards, pregnant women who wish to do so should have the right to transfer to non-VDU work during the course of their pregnancy without loss of pay, status or career prospects.'

Repetition strain injury (RSI) is the term for a range of injuries associated historically with production-line jobs involving intensive, repetitive or forceful work. However, since the introduction of new technology into offices, particularly in the form of the electronic keyboard which allows for very rapid keystroking, RSI can be found in the office as well as the factory.

The medical terms for the different types of RSI include tenosynovitis (teno), tendinitis, epicondylitis, carpal tunnel syndrome, writers' cramp and static muscle strain.

RSI is always painful. Although it is completely preventable, if the conditions which cause it are not improved while the disease is in its early stages it can lead to irreversible damage and disability. The London Hazards Centre's 1988 booklet on RSI gives detailed advice on recognising and preventing it.[12]

RSI is now well recognised in Australia and trade unions there have campaigned against it widely. Realising that many data processors key over 12,000 strokes an hour, a slogan has been coined: 'You can leave production targets at work, pain goes home with you. Go Safe. Go 10,000.' It should be pointed out though that there is as yet no proof that keying 10,000 strokes an hour is a safe level. A new standard for VDU ergonomics proposed by the British Standards Institution gives some useful information on the standards for VDU equipment and for design of VDU work.[13]

The most important conclusion that can be drawn from investigations into the health hazards of VDU work is that they must always start from the point of the actual experiences of operators themselves. If deteriorating eyesight, RSI, depression and anxiety are being widely experienced, then it simply isn't good enough for employers to cite medical opinions which suggest that the dangers do not exist. It is also particularly unsatisfactory if undeniable 'evidence' has to take the form of irrevocable damage to employees' health. The crucial thing is to prevent injury and permanent disability by intervening before it is too late.

The London Hazards Centre's 1987 book on VDU hazards provides some useful guidance for VDU workers trying to organise improvements in both job and workplace design.[14]

Can the Law Help?

Trade unions, faced these days with constraints on their ability to organise, have become more active in using legislation to pursue workers' interests. The equal value legislation which was forced on the British government by the European Community is a good example of this. Even though it is widely recognised that the legislation is cumbersome and is extremely difficult to win successful equal value claims by, there have been some important successes fought in the courts. The 1989 decision by the Law Lords in favour of Rene Pickstone, a warehouse checker at Freemans, who although working mainly with women, did have a few token men doing the same job as her, will be of significance to office workers who often have a handful of men doing the same jobs as them.

The EC has drafted a directive which aims to set minimum safety and health requirements for work with VDUs. Unfortunately resistance by the British government to it seems to make this unlikely to become law.[15] (The articles are set out in Appendix II.)

Although the wording is sometimes vague and includes let-out phrases like 'in so far as is reasonably possible', the articles and annex do provide some back-up for demanding that employers both test for bad effects on employees' health and take remedial action if hazards are discovered. *The most significant absence from the directive is any reference to length of time during the working day to be spent on VDU work or requirements for rest pauses.* There would no doubt be an enormous struggle between member states over exactly what should be legislated if this were included. However, by omitting any direct reference to this central issue, the directive becomes very much a backcloth for workers' health and safety demands, rather than a determination of any positive outcome. Without office staff insisting on interpreting the directive and detailing its implications for the work they do, it could become something that any employer can profess to follow without necessarily having to introduce any safeguards into the office.

What is to be Done?

The TUC guidelines which have been mentioned a number of times in this chapter provide a very helpful guidance to negotiators and cover in detail a large range of health and safety issues raised by new technology. In the introduction a significant proviso is put:

> The trade union movement has devoted a great deal of effort into developing policies . . . [which] deal with a very wide range of problems: avoiding the destruction of jobs, improving the content of work, creating a better work environment, etc. These VDU guidelines have a much more restricted objective. They are concerned purely with the health, safety and ergonomic problems which arise as a result of the operation of visual display units.(pp. 9–10)

Putting this limitation on health and safety questions ultimately involves some sort of backing away from fundamental issues about work organisation and office hierarchies. Julia Stallibrass points out in a NALGO research publication, 'Mixed work for data preparation operators' (August 1986) that despite a doubling of the proportion of NALGO branches which have achieved rest-breaks and restrictions on total hours of VDU work, there are still reports of data preparation operators working full-time on VDUs. Implementing these agreements, which are anyway the necessary starting point for protecting operators' health, does not only require a 'union-minded' workforce. It means changing the way jobs are created and skills encouraged or denied. It means making demands that will shake up the division of work in the office in such a way as to put a question mark over the very existence of 'VDU operator' or 'Data Prep operator' jobs. Anything less is like fighting a forest fire with a very leaky bucket.

Checklist

1 Why does your employer use computers?
2 Do people complain of problems when using VDUs?
3 Do you have enough breaks when using a VDU?
4 Have people who use VDUs had their eyes tested recently?
5 Can people who are thinking of starting a family transfer to non-VDU work if they want to?
6 Do people complain of aches and pains when doing a lot of keyboard work?
7 Do some keyboard operators key more than 10,000 strokes an hour?
8 Were you and your colleagues consulted about the computer equipment, its purpose and design and siting in the office?

Notes

1 *New Technology: A Health and Safety Report* (APEX, February 1985), p. 65.
2 *Computing*, 29 April 1982.
3 *A Question of Earnings* (London Equal Value Steering Group, 1987).
4 London Hazards Centre, 'RSI epidemic in the workplace', *Daily Hazard*, No. 21, April 1989, p. 1.
5 TUC, *Guidelines on VDUs* (London, 1985).
6 *VDUs, Health and Jobs* (LRD, 1985).

7 'CPSA's survey of British Telecom's Bristol Computer Centre', in *Health and Safety at Work*, December 1984.

8 D. Albury, T. Butler and M. Craig, *Visual Display Units Health and Safety Survey* (NELPCO, September 1986), p. 46.

9 Ursula Huws, *VDU Hazards Handbook – A Worker's Guide to the Effects of New Technology* (London Hazards Centre Trust Limited, 1987).

10 Health and Safety Executive, *Working with VDUs* (HSE, 1986), p. 2

11 'EPI study links VDT use to increased miscarriage risk', *VDT News*, Vol. v, No. 4, July/August 1988.

12 London Hazards Centre, *Repetition Strain Injuries – Hidden Harm from Overuse* (London Hazards Centre Trust Limited, January 1988).

13 British Standards Institution, *Draft British Standard Recommendations for Ergonomic Requirements for Design and Use of Visual Display Terminals in Offices* (BSI, 1987).

14 Huws, op. cit.

15 'Pressing the key to VDU safety', *Labour Research*, June 1989.

5
Changing the Deal

This is a time of high unemployment and weakened employment rights. Being out of work means facing continuous pressure from the state to prove you are actively looking for a job or accept a badly paid one with poor conditions of work or otherwise face losing your rights to welfare benefits. This may hardly seem to be a context in which office workers can expect to force their employers to eliminate workplace hazards. Actively creating healthy and beneficial working conditions appears an even more remote possibility. However there are both legal and trade union means which can still provide some protection as well as a basis for organising a change in the terms of the deal you are being offered at work.

This chapter covers the law relating to health and safety at work and the rights trade union representatives have. Whatever the letter of the law, you are in a much better position to make sure it's put into practice and to push for higher standards than the minimum set (particularly when this is not spelt out) when you are in a trade union which is recognised by your employer. There are suggestions for ways of tackling work hazards which can ensure you are facing your boss as a group of workers rather than challenging the situation as a lone and vulnerable individual who could be sacked for questioning management's right to manage.

How the Law Developed

It has taken an extraordinary length of time to get the level of health and safety legislation we have now for office workers, which nevertheless still contains loopholes and is often weakly enforced. Even when laws are broken and employers brought to court they can be fined derisory amounts which hardly dent their profit margins. After the Second World War the Gower Committee was set up to enquire into office conditions and its

Report recommended that there should be state provision for health, welfare and safety in non-industrial employment. Legislation covering factories has been in place since the nineteenth century, yet it took another two decades for an Act to be passed on offices, in 1963.

The Offices, Shops and Railway Premises Act (OSRPA) 1963 includes requirements for cleanliness, avoidance of overcrowding, maintenance of a 'reasonable temperature', provision of 'adequate ventilation and guarding and adequate lighting' and provision of sanitary and washing and first aid facilities. The Act is, on the one hand, specific – it lists particular requirements – and on the other, vague. It uses words like 'adequate' and 'reasonable' to define standards. Nevertheless, parts of the Act are very useful and sometimes strongly worded, such as the section on ventilation.

The Factories Act 1961, which brought together all the hundreds of bits and pieces of legislation, is worth perusing. You may find you can 'borrow' a section and apply it to your situation. Borrowing from the Codes of Practice and Guidance Notes is useful for backing up a case, but doesn't have the force of law. Codes of Practice (e.g. on noise) are used by health and safety inspectors to *persuade* employers to comply. Guidance Notes are issued on various processes and substances and, while not legally binding, provide useful ammunition in negotiations. Push your employer to supply you with a copy of *Redgrave's Guides* to the Factories Act and to OSRPA. *Redgrave's Guides* give summaries of these Acts and all the regulations made under them, together with interpretations based on legal cases, and there are helpful indexes.

All health and safety legislation now comes under the umbrella of the *Health and Safety at Work Act 1974* (HASAWA). This Act is based on the philosophy and recommendations of the Robens Committee, which considered that too much law existed and that this was responsible for the 'apathy' about health issues at work. The conclusion was that simpler law was required and that results could only be achieved by cooperation between employer and employee. This approach was preferred to greater legal coercion. One of the most significant regulations made under this Act gave rights to trade union representatives (see below). This again underlines the usefulness of a unionised workplace and the possibility of pressing for changes without simply relying on court cases.

The HASAWA re-organised all the legislation and applies to people, not places. Everyone who works is now covered. This Act places on employers a *statutory duty* to ensure, so far as is reasonably practicable, the safety and health and welfare of their employees at work. The qualifying phrase 'as far as is reasonably practicable' is a loophole. It means that in court employers can argue that they cannot afford to make the required improvement, e.g. to make the officer quieter. Economic criteria are legally acceptable. Risks are balanced: profit versus health. Where a piece of legislation is not weakened by such a phrase as in the following section from OSRPA, you are on very strong ground:

> Effective and suitable provision *shall be made* for securing and maintaining, by the circulation of adequate supplies of fresh or artificially purified air, the ventilation of every room . . . (section 7(1))

What the Health and Safety at Work Act Says

Some sections of the HASAWA are of particular interest here and deserve a brief summary.

Section 1 states the aims of the Act:

a maintaining or improving standards of health, safety and welfare of people at work;
b protecting other people against risks to health and safety arising out of work activities;
c controlling the storage and use of dangerous substances;
d controlling certain emissions into the air from certain premises.

Section 2 puts a general duty on employers to ensure the safety, health and welfare at work of their employees; to consult them concerning arrangements for joint action on health and safety matters; in certain circumstances, at the request of duly appointed or elected trade union safety representatives, to establish safety committees; and to prepare and publicise a written statement of their safety policy and arrangements.

Section 2(2) is at the heart of this Act, and its requirements potentially cover all hazards and risks to health. It covers the following aspects:

a Plant systems of work must be provided and maintained so as to be safe and without risk to health.
b Articles and substances must be used, handled, stored and transported in a safe and healthy way.
c Employees must be provided with information, instruction, training and supervision.
d A place of work must be safe, with safe access and egress.
e The working environment must be safe and healthy, and adequate welfare arrangements are required.

Section 6 places duties on anyone who designs, manufactures, imports or supplies an article or substance for use at work to ensure, so far as it is under their control, that the article or substance is safe when used in accordance with information supplied by them. The duty extends to the provision of necessary information and the carrying out of necessary testing, inspection and research. Those who install plant are also to have a duty to ensure that it is safely installed.

Section 7 places duties on employees to take reasonable care to ensure that they do not endanger themselves or anyone else who may be affected by their work activities; and to cooperate with employers and others in meeting statutory requirements. *This is a favourite section with employers, usually emphasised at the top of their policy statement, the implication being that you cause accidents and disease. This section can also be interpreted to mean that you have a right to refuse to do a job that could potentially damage your health, e.g. not operate a VDU that's hurting your eyes.*

Section 9 provides that no employer may charge his employees for anything done or equipment provided for health and safety purposes under a statutory requirement.

Section 79 lays down that in their annual reports to shareholders, directors will be required to give information about what their companies are doing in safety and health matters.

The Regulations on Safety Representatives and Safety Committees

Regulations are made under the Acts and add more detailed requirements. These may cover particular hazards (e.g. first aid) or industries (e.g. foundries). They have the same force as the law under which they are made. The HASAWA, OSRPA and

Factories Act, together with the regulations made under them, are *criminal law*, and breaches by employers are punishable by fines or imprisonment.

Under section 2 of the HASAWA regulations which came into force in October 1978 provisions were made for workers' inspectors to be elected by trade unionists in every workplace. They give workers unprecedented legal rights and powers in the sphere of health and safety at work. Safety representatives have the right to investigate complaints and hazards, causes of ill-nesses and accidents; the right to inspect the workplace; the right to know, by obtaining information on substances, pro-cesses, surveys and measurements; the right to take up problems with management. They have a right to time off, training and facilities to do the job. Safety reps are not legally liable for accidents or ill-health if the law is broken. The regulations also make provisions for the setting up of safety committees where union and management agree they are desirable.

Safety reps are elected by the trade union membership and must be clearly distinguished from the safety officer, who is paid by the employer and is part of management. The union branch decides how many and which areas they represent and their appointment or removal is *totally* a matter for the union. They have more legal right than shop stewards, although in some unions the same person doubles up as shop steward and safety rep. A Labour Research Department survey in March 1984 of 4314 safety reps covering 272,480 workers, showed an average ratio of 1 rep: 63 employees (range 1:30 to 1:150).

Any employer who does not give the following rights to safety reps is committing a criminal offence and can be prosecuted.

1 The right to investigate members' complaints, potential hazards, dangerous occurrences or near-misses, causes of accidents and health problems. One very useful way of carrying out investi-gations is to draw up a short questionnaire and to carry out your own health survey in the office. A model questionnaire is given later.

2 The right to inspect the workplace. Following the regulations these inspections should be made as and when necessary. Inspec-tion should be carried out after an accident or 'near-miss', and after the publication of any relevant Health and Safety Executive documents or trade union information. To help carry out inspec-tions, it is useful to have checklists. You can get plans to help

you work out areas for inspection from the fire certificate, a copy of which management must give you.

3 The right to information. The information safety reps can legally demand is very widely defined and includes information concerning:

a plans, performance and any proposed changes concerning the organisation of the workplace;

b technical information concerning the hazards and precautions of machinery, equipment, processes and substances in use at work;

c accident and health/sickness records;

d results of measurements and surveys.

This right to information includes communication from employers, manufacturers and inspectors.

4 The right to facilities. To do the job of safety rep you'll need some facilities. The regulations don't specify what these are, but the TUC recommends a room and desk, filing cabinet, access to telephone and internal mailing system, typing and duplication facilities and use of a notice board. You will also need a library of books and pamphlets. You may want to negotiate things like the provision of a room for meetings of safety reps and other union reps. It is also possible to negotiate paid time off work for safety reps to meet. In 1982 an Industrial Tribunal[1] ruled that NALGO had a 'well-founded' complaint when the London Borough of Haringey refused paid time off for a meeting of all its safety reps. Subsequently, the Council agreed to give three hours a month for the union's Health and Safety Committee to meet.

5 The right to training. If your employer arranges health and safety courses you can go on these, but they are no substitute for TUC courses. Your regional TUC Education Office will send you a form. Employers must give reps time off with pay to go on TUC union courses. These are usually ten-week courses, one day a week, organised by the TUC, but some unions do their own courses, e.g. MSF, GMB and NALGO, which are useful in addition to the basic course.

You could also try to negotiate health and safety training for all members in addition to union representatives. And where possible negotiate cover for reps attending courses so they don't come back to find a pile of work waiting for them.

6 The right to make representations to management on behalf of your members. If you make a complaint, make sure you insist on a time-limit for a rectification of the fault so that some action

can follow. Employers' safety policies should be clear on whom to complain to.

There is a number of examples of successful actions by safety reps, ranging from getting a second first-aid room for women away from the industrial section of the press at Butterworths to banning the use of *Tippex 4010* and thinner.[2]

Haringey NALGO succeeded in negotiating a safe working practice code for photocopiers, and the CPSA at the British Telecom Data Processing Executive in Bristol negotiated an agreement for VDU users in May 1984. It included the right to come off VDU work for pregnant women, no productivity measures, installing air extractors, new chairs and footrests, and filters to be fitted to the screens. ASTMS (now MSF) at Ilford Ltd, in Cheshire, helped set up safe working practices to protect against possible chemical hazards affecting the skin. APEX at the Society for Civil and Public Servants in London got fire regulations enforced and first aiders appointed with a first aid room. They also ensured that a cervical cancer screening unit should visit the workplace.

It is clear from these examples that battles can be won and significant improvements introduced which protect workers' health. Simply having the right in law to monitor health and safety and to push for changes is not enough. Well-informed and active safety reps who are listening to their members and encouraging them to consider safety issues, are a key element in outlawing work hazards.

Management Safety Committees

These have both management and union representation and guidelines for them are laid down in the Regulations. You don't have to have one and if you consider it ineffective, you can always withdraw from it. Management safety committees are the traditional way of dealing with health and safety – the issue is shelved and then wheeled out once every six months to be discussed in a desultory way over tea and biscuits. There is much more recognition in trade unions now that health and safety is a conflict issue that needs to be bargained over. How much you will win depends on how strong you are. You can't begin to negotiate better conditions in tired committees. But in your situation you may feel you could use a committee in some way.

You may wish to push for a new committee or re-organise the old one. If so, make sure there are equal numbers of management and union reps on it, and that there is someone on it from management who can *take decisions* there and then, especially regarding finances. Otherwise it will always remain a talking shop. The employer must set up a committee if two or more safety reps ask for one and must consult the reps about setting one up.

Enforcing Health and Safety Legislation

Health and safety inspectors together with local authority environmental health inspectors are employed to police Britain's workplaces. However, given the Conservative government's policies, since coming to power in 1979, of cutting public spending, many local authorities are seriously understaffed in their environmental health departments. And total HSE staff have dropped from 4229 in 1979 to 3682 in 1989.

If your workplace is a private office block or an office that's part of a shop, your inspector will probably be from the local authority. You can contact her or him through your local town hall. If your office is in a factory or in local government or Crown property, the inspector will probably be from the Health and Safety Executive (HSE).

The HSE is the collective name given to the inspectors, scientists and administrative staff working for it. It is divided into 21 area offices. Prior to the HASAWA, HSE inspectors used to be known as factory inspectors. They can enter premises, inspect and investigate, take samples, examine documents, seize and destroy articles or substances that may cause serious injury. They must give information to union reps, such as on hazards or tests and details of what he or she has asked the employer to do.

Inspectors can issue *Improvement Notices* warning employers that they have 21 days or more to comply with the law. (These notices can be ignored during appeal.) *Prohibition Notices* are much stronger and require an immediate halt to the work activity if the inspector believes there to be an imminent danger. However, the inspectors are overworked and unable comprehensively to cover each workplace. In fact, it has been estimated that on average they only inspect a workplace every nine years. If you aren't in a trade union which has recognition from your employer, they are a resource to turn to. But if you are union-ised, your safety reps have the right regularly to inspect your workplace and are likely to be far more effective.

Inspectors rarely prosecute. In line with the tone of the HASAWA and its emphasis on a cooperative approach to health and safety issues, they tend to opt for persuasion and guidance. Even when they do prosecute, the court may fail to impose heavy fines on employers. Average fines are still only around £100, although fines of up to £1000 can be levied and managers can be imprisoned for up to two years.

Some inspectors may be sympathetic to trade unionists, but are hampered by layers of bureaucracy and cuts in their resources.

As the recession deepened during the year, industrial and commercial management became increasingly occupied with economic survival and thus, among other strategies, inevitably reviewed the financial impact of occupational health and safety requirements. Inspectors too were compelled to con-sider their requirements in the same light.[3]

Even if you are disappointed with the response of an inspector brought into your workplace, complaining and keeping the pres-sure on can and does work. Office workers in the Social Services Department in Handsworth, Birmingham, were seriously over-crowded. They called in an inspector who eventually issued an Improvement Notice and warned the authorities that they would be fined £1000 if better accommodation were not found within three months. A further £100 fine *per day* would be levied after that if no action was taken. Management agreed to install a Portakabin and move workers to a new building as soon as possible.

The HSE inspector told the NUPE branch chairperson that they rarely visited local authority premises *unless safety represen-tatives* called them in.

If you work on Crown property (e.g. in the civil service) the inspectors cannot enforce the health and safety legislation. Crown immunity means that they can't be prosecuted. Inspec-tors can, and do, inspect Crown properties and issue Crown Improvement and Prohibition Notices. The relevant government departments have given an undertaking that they will meet the requirements of the HASAWA and, of course, persons in the public service of the Crown can be prosecuted. The 1981 Health and Safety at Work *Manufacturing and Service Industries* report notes: 'Crown Notices are being used increasingly', and that 'In spite of the status of Crown privilege held by Health Authorities, Crown Notices are an effective instrument of enforcement.' However, in 1986 Crown immunity for health and safety regulations in hospitals and other NHS establishments was lifted and this may pave the way for the lifting of immunity in other Crown premises.

The *Health and Safety Commission* is at the head of government administration on health and safety. It is made up of representatives from the TUC, CBI and local authorities. This tripartite body is responsible for research, information, setting up inquiries, proposing regulations and approving codes of practice. It makes decisions on such things as the levels of dangerous substances that will be permissible for us to breathe at work – 'as far as is reasonably practicable'.

The *Employment Medical Advisory Service* (EMAS) is the medical wing of the HSE. One of its functions is to give workers 'information and advice on health in relation to employment'. EMAS employ doctors and have regional offices. You can try calling them in for occupational health problems. But it's worth being cautious as some of these are part-time company doctors.

Compensation, Benefits and Tribunals

The advantages of trade union membership are very clear in this area, whether it's ensuring that you get advice and support through an industrial tribunal or meaning you are accompanied by a safety rep whenever being interviewed by management in relation to an accident which could lead to compensation.

The legal machine is very complicated – it almost looks as if it was constructed to make things difficult. If you have an accident or are exposed to a dangerous substance, report it. Make sure it is recorded in the accident book. This protects you later.

If you are injured at work or become ill as a result of inadequate safety precautions, you can sue your employer for damages. You will need legal help for this and should ask your trade union to help you get a lawyer. Or your local Citizens' Advice Bureau or Law Centre will help. Widows and other dependants of people killed at work can also claim damages. It may take several years for this kind of action to be finalised. Only 20 per cent of cases are successful, and most cases are settled out of court.[4] Take a copy of every relevant scrap of paper. If applying, you will need full support from your fellow workers to follow the labyrinth of forms and tribunals.

If you are off work because of sickness or injury there are three ways of getting money. Statutory Sick Pay (SSP), paid by the employer, was introduced in 1983. The employer claims back the cost from the government. Everyone paying National Insurance contributions gets SSP for up to eight weeks in any year. Sickness Benefit can be claimed from the DSS if you are not entitled to SSP. Finally, there are occupational sick pay schemes which are paid by the employer and will have been negotiated by your trade union. The TUC recommends unions to negotiate sick pay schemes whereby full earnings are paid during sickness absence.

Gaining More Health Protection than the Legal Minimum

Where you do have basic rights, as in the realm of health and safety, it is essential to know what those rights are and fight to get more. If you know what the law says, your boss will find it difficult to confuse you by telling you that you don't have a legal right to certain things. But as pointed out in a National Council for Civil Liberties publication:

> In a unionised workplace the union normally succeeds in negotiating much more favourable conditions for the workers than the law provides. In cases of dispute between workers and employers – for instance, involving discipline, dismissal or redundancy – the law is only a last resort. Many employers, as well as the unions, prefer to reach an agreed settlement of a dispute through the normal industrial relations, rather than using expensive, cumbersome legal machinery.[5]

A strong, effective union is your best protection from health hazards. If you are not a union member, you should contact your local Trades Council or contact directly one of the white-collar unions listed in Appendix I. If your workplace isn't unionised, discuss the matter with fellow workers and perhaps arrange a meeting outside working hours at which an official from the local office of a union can speak. You can also get leaflets from unions to distribute at work.

Your trade union should be recognised by the employer for the purposes of negotiating pay and other conditions, protecting health and safety, negotiating disciplinary procedures, negotiating pension schemes, and so on. If your workplace is newly organised, the union will have to apply for recognition. This will be done by the steward elected by the union members in the workplace, with the help of the full-time union official.

Members of a recognised union are entitled to time off for union activities (e.g. to vote or to attend a meeting of an outside body as a union representative, or to attend an executive committee meeting or annual conference of the union as a branch delegate). Time off does not have to be given for normal branch meetings except where the matter to be discussed is urgent. The employer is not obliged to pay workers for time off for union activities, although the union can negotiate for payment to be made. Lay officials of a recognised union – shop stewards, branch secretaries, safety reps – are entitled to paid time off for union activities and for relevant training approved by the TUC or union.

Historically, unions have had to struggle hard to gain decent wages and the right to organise at all. In the early part of the century, clerks were automatically sacked if they tried to claim overtime pay. There are still attempts to victimise office workers who try to improve their working conditions. It is unlawful for an employer to victimise any worker for trying to join a trade union. If you think your employer may do so, or if you are threatened with dismissal, you should join a trade union immediately and discuss the position with the local official. But be very careful not to let your boss know. If you are sacked before other workers have joined the union, you have very little chance of getting your job back because there will be no workplace organisation to support you. Any meetings with the union must be outside working hours, or the employer will complain that you are spending time on an unauthorised activity.

Make a complaint of victimisation to the industrial tribunal. This must be done within seven days, and you will need a certificate from the union's full-time official. All workers are protected against victimisation for joining or trying to join a union, including part-time workers, and people who have only just started working for the firm.

Unions that represent office workers have become increasingly concerned about work hazards, particularly given the widespread introduction of VDU working. There are also groups of office workers which bring out regular bulletins such as the VDU Workers Rights Group or Redder Tape. Unions are only as strong as their membership and it is you who are experiencing at first hand the conditions of work in your office. You are in the best position to know if anything is wrong and what needs changing. Your union will be able to give you advice and back you up, but the impetus for organising must come from the office workers themselves.

First Steps in Tackling Health Hazards

A very good way of simultaneously raising health and safety issues in the office and getting information that can be used in arguing with management is to organise a health survey. Using a questionnaire such as the following may reveal some startling facts about the symptoms being widely experienced.

1 Name (optional)
2 Department/Area
3 Age group:
under 21
21–30
31–45
46–55
Over 55
4 Sex
5 Which of these categories describes your health?
Excellent
Good
Average
Bad
6 Do you suffer from any of the following while on the job?
Digestive disorders   Often   Sometimes   Never
Eyestrain
Headaches
Tension, e.g. digestive
Tiredness
Sore throat
Sore eyes
Stiff shoulders or neck
Backache
Nausea
Skin rashes
Varicose veins
Bad chest
Other
Please give further details if you wish
7 Do you find you have more or fewer absences from work on
account of transient illness, e.g. colds, headaches, 'flu, since
starting this job?
More
Less
About the same
8 Do you visit your doctor more or less frequently since starting
here?
More
Less
About the same

 9 Do you know what, if anything, your doctor has diagnosed?
    Yes
    No
    Can you give details?
10 What are the health and safety problems that most affect
    you?
11 Eyes and eyesight
    Do your eyes bother you?
    What do you think the cause is?
12 Do you wear glasses or contact lenses?
    Yes
    No
    Did you wear them before you started work here?
    Yes
    No
13 Do you feel there has been a deterioration in your eyesight
    since starting your present job?
    Yes
    No
14 If so, what do you think the cause(s) is (are)?
15 Headaches
    Do your headaches occur mainly inside or outside working
    hours?
    Outside
    Inside
    Both
16 Do they generally occur at a particular time?
    Morning
    Midday
    Afternoon
    Evening
    No specific time
17 Do you think any of these factors contribute to your head-
    aches? (please tick)

	Yes	No	Perhaps
Stress			
Lighting			
Air conditioning			
Smoke in atmosphere			
Chemical fumes			
Noise			
Other (please specify)			

---

18 Fertility hazards
Have you ever suffered any of the following symptoms while
at work?

	Yes	No
Irregular periods		
Miscarriage		
Other childbirth-related problems		
Sterility		

Once you have got answers to these questions it will be possible to start trying to link any symptoms with their causes and
then demand changes to working practices, office equipment or
office accommodation.

It is possible for trade unions to negotiate a *safety agreement*
which spells out rights to be consulted and advised *prior to any
change* in working conditions. This is a powerful right which
exists in law but is often not exercised. An agreement could
incorporate more than the legislation offers, for instance:

1 The right to stop the job: this is conspicuously absent from the
legislation, although it exists as a legal right for safety reps in
Sweden.
2 The right to have outside advisers of the reps' choice on the
office or shop floor, to take samples, make recommendations,
etc.
3 Internal prohibition and improvement notices to be issued in
the way the Health and Safety Inspectors issue them. If a process
or product is held to be unsafe, the reps issue a notice saying
that specific improvements must be made by a given date, or
that the use of a given unsafe process is prohibited until further
notice. The notices are signed by both union and management
sides.

Strategies for Improving Workplace Safety

From 1 January 1990 an employer may not carry on any work
which is liable to expose workers to any substance hazardous to
health unless a suitable and sufficient assessment has been made
of the risk to health, and of the steps which need to be taken
to eliminate or control workers' exposure to these substances.
The London Hazards Centre's fact sheet on COSHH, sections

of which are reproduced below, summarises the new regulations and shows how they may be used to control hazardous substances in your workplace.[6]

The three key ways of tackling any hazard at work mean *assessing it, monitoring exposure, and controlling*. A good safety agreement means you're half-way there. But when management doesn't keep to the agreement or pressure is needed, you may face the necessity for direct action. This could range from refusing to take telephone calls, withdrawing 'goodwill' (not making the coffee), campaigning through the press, lightning stoppages or all-out strikes. It's worth remembering that while 16 million working days are lost a year because of accidents and ill health, during 1983, for instance, only 3.8 million days were lost through strikes. You may after all even be doing management a favour by striking if this removes a workplace hazard which is making the workforce ill.

The Control of Substances Hazardous to Health

COSHH regulations are the most important piece of health and safety law since the Health and Safety at Work Act. The regulations became law in October 1989 though employers had until 1 January 1990 to comply with most provisions. Thanks to employers' efforts the COSHH Regulations are not as strong as they should be, but it is up to safety reps to use the strengths and minimise the weaknesses.

COSHH covers all workplaces where substances hazardous to health are used or arise as by-products. These substances come in a variety of forms, including pastes, powders, liquids, oils, gases, aerosols, sprays, fumes, dusts, bacteria or viruses. They could arise as solvents, glues, oils, resins, paints, pesticides, acids, degreasers, thinners, toxic metals, welding fumes, cleaning materials, man-made mineral fibres, inks and many more.

Substances exempt from COSHH are asbestos and lead. Risks not covered are ionising radiation, fire, explosion and pressurisation.

Employers' Legal Duties under COSHH

Assessment (Regulation 6)

Assessment means asking the right questions and getting accurate answers.

- What substances are in use (stored, transported or disposed of) in the workplace, or can arise in the work process?
- Are any of these substances hazardous to health?
- Is anyone at work exposed to these substances?
- What further steps are needed to get clear answers so that action on control can be taken? (e.g. do we need specialists?)

The approved code on COSHH assessments states that records must be made and kept for virtually all assessments. They should contain sufficient information to show how decisions about risks and precautions were arrived at; reflect the detail with which the assessment was carried out; be useful and meaningful to those who will need to know about it, now and subsequently; and indicate the circumstances when the assessment might need to be reviewed.

Safety reps need to be involved at all stages. The trade union right to consultation is ensured under the Health and Safety at Work Act, Section 2 (6), by which employers must consult safety reps on all health and safety matters. The Safety Reps Regulations 7 (2) requires the employer to provide information on 'plans' which affect health and safety matters.

Control (Regulation 7)

The employer must ensure that the exposure of workers to substances hazardous to health is either prevented or, where this is not reasonably practicable, adequately controlled. This applies whether the substance is hazardous through inhalation, ingestion, absorption through the skin or contact with the skin.

Exposure must be prevented by:

1 Removing the hazardous substance by changing the process.
2 Substituting with a safer substance, or using it in a safer form (e.g. pastes instead of sprays).

Or where this is not reasonably practicable:

3 Totally enclosing the process.
4 Using partial enclosure and extract ventilation equipment.
5 Using safe systems of work and personal protective equipment.

Only if one method is considered to be 'not reasonably practicable' should the next one be considered, though a combination of control measures can be used.

Personal protective equipment is to be used only as a last resort, or as a stop-gap till proper control measures can be implemented.

Every employer who provides any control measure should ensure that it is fully and properly used.

Monitoring of Exposure (Regulation 10)

Employers should carry out tests to see that levels of substances are within safe limits. This can be done by general air monitoring, and by workers wearing personal samplers to measure their exposure as they work. It must be done if failure or deterioration of the control measures could result in serious risk to health, or where the substances have a maximum exposure limit or occupational exposure standard which must not be exceeded. A record must be kept showing dates, procedures and results.

Information, Instruction and Training For Persons Who May Be Exposed to Substances Hazardous to Health (Regulation 12)

Any workers likely to be exposed must be given information and training about the dangers of their work, and ways of avoiding those dangers. They must also be given information on the results of environmental monitoring or medical tests that have been carried out by their employer.

What Can Safety Reps Do?

Make demands for training and guidance from your union. The TUC is to produce a full policy document, a booklet and leaflets aimed at both safety reps and members. They are also developing COSHH workshops to train safety reps – so make sure you take full advantage of them.

Check to see what action is being planned at your workplace:

- Has a complete audit of substances been carried out?
- Are assessments underway now on those substances identified as hazardous to health?
- Has a central point been set up to collect and review all information?
- Get copies of all your employer's information.

- Report all your members' health complaints in writing.
- Use your rights to investigate, inspect and consult with your members.

Inform Others

If you get some information on workplace hazards, make sure other workers get to know about it. You could try using the local press and informing your union branch and health and safety officer.

One thing you'll be up against time and again will be the argument that there is no money for what you are demanding. Whether it's cutbacks in public expenditure or the firm going to the wall, management will centre their resistance on the financial implications. Apart from pointing out to them that they are taking an extremely short-term view because allowing workplace hazards to continue will lead to staff on sick leave or claims for compensation against the organisation, you also need to hold firm to the position that health is a priority. No one should be forced to do a job that is potentially or actually causing serious damage to their health.

Healthy and safe working conditions will not be won without a fight. In the present context of a government aiming to dismantle the welfare state and privatise every aspect of collective provision, whether it's pensions, the water supply, housing or the National Health Service, the struggle has a sharp edge to it. If the battle is lost at work, there is very little left to pick up the pieces. However, workers do succeed in getting their management to change equipment and work processes and to recognise the impossibility of gaining staff cooperation unless they are informed and included in decision-making. Even when the victory is an apparently small one, it can act to turn the tide in a workplace where workers have for years had to put up with unsatisfactory and dangerous working practices. And anything you gain can set a precedent or be an encouragement to other staff in different workplaces or employed by different bosses – something that managers are all too aware of and which goes some way to explaining their obstinacy in the face of the good sense you are talking.

Checklist

1 Is the law on office safety on the wall in your office?
2 Have you or your colleagues been on a health and safety course?
3 Have you thought of starting a union at your office?
4 If you have a union, have you elected safety reps?
5 Do your safety reps know their rights? Have they been trained? Do they inspect your office? Do they report back to you and your colleagues?
6 Do you have a joint union-management safety committee at your office?
7 Do you know the name, address and phone number of your local council Environmental Health Officer (EHO)?
8 Has the local council EHO inspected your office? Have you seen a copy of her/his report?
9 Have you contacted your local union office/official/hazards centre/advice centre for help?
10 If you or a colleague has had an accident, did you contact a solicitor (via your union if you are in one) to see if a claim for negligence is possible against your employer's insurance?
11 Does your employer display her or his certificate of employer's liability insurance?
12 Have you thought of carrying out a health survey of your office colleagues?

Notes

1 See *Labour Research*, May 1983.
2 As Keith Puttick, Father of the Chapel at Butterworths in London, explained: 'Members here believe that these whiteners can and do affect their health and for that reason we have stopped using them. . . . Steps have been taken to extend the ban in the rest of IPC and other journalistic and editorial areas. We have asked the company to cease supplies of these whiteners into the company and this is what we expect them to do.' *Safety Reps in Action* (Labour Research Department, November 1984), p. 28.
3 Health and Safety Executive, *Manufacturing and Services Industries 1980 – A Report of the Work of HM Factory Inspectorate* (HMSO, 1982).
4 See Pat Kinnersly, *The Hazards of Work* (London, Pluto Press, 1977), chapter 11: 'Winning damages'.

5 B. Birtler and P. Hewitt, *Your Rights at Work*, third edition (NCCL, 1983), p. 5.

6 London Hazards Centre, 'Control of hazardous substances factsheet', *Daily Hazard*, No. 24, London Hazards Centre, December 1989.

Appendix I
Trade Union-won Provisions for Working with VDUs

ASTMS, now MSF

Maximum two hours, with half an hour break. Maximum work in any day should be no more than four hours. Shorter work periods with a greater number of breaks are advisable, e.g. 50 minutes' work followed by a 15-minute break. All breaks should be taken away from the work station.

CPSA

At the Post Office, CPSA members have agreed a code of practice whereby normal time spent with VDUs is 100 minutes a day maximum (180 minutes during abnormal work peaks). No operator is required to work more than 50 minutes continuously without a break of at least 15 minutes.

TUC printing industries committee

Minimum of 30 minutes' break from the screen in each period of two hours' continuous work, and there should be an agreed maximum of work on the screen during any one shift. Whenever possible the work pattern should be programmed so that periods of work at the VDU alternate with periods which give the eyes an opportunity to become restored.

APEX

Twenty minutes' rest in every hour for operators involved in continuous VDU work throughout the day. Wherever possible the work pattern should be arranged so that periods of work at the VDU are alternated with periods which give the eyes an opportunity to become restored.

AUEW/TASS

Maximum of four hours' work at a VDU during a working day. Regular breaks from screen working are essential – at least twenty minutes' break in each period of two hours' continuous working.

GMB

All workers should have regular fixed work breaks away from the display unit, preferably every hour. If it is inconvenient for the worker to leave his [!] work station on a regular basis, there should be provision for the display screen to be turned off or made dark at regular intervals.

BIFU

There should be an agreed maximum period of operation of VDUs during any one shift: this maximum will depend on the concentration needed in any one task. However, the following should be observed:

a the operators must work *no longer* than two hours continuously at a VDU;
b the relief period between spells of work on a VDU must be no less than thirty minutes.

Appendix II
Draft EC
Guidelines on Work
with VDUs

The draft guidelines have been through several stages and the following summary incorporates the amended proposals, most of which are likely to be included in the version scheduled for implementation in June 1990.

Selected paragraphs from the introductory statements in the Directive are reproduced below:

Whereas Article 118A of the Treaty [establishing the European Economic Community] provides that the Council shall adopt, by means of directives, minimum requirements designed to encourage improvements, especially in the working environment, to ensure better protection of the safety and health of workers;

Whereas compliance with the minimum requirements for ensuring a better level of safety at workstations with VDUs is essential for ensuring the safety and health of workers and whereas these requirements are also essential to promote fair competition;

Whereas employers must keep abreast of technological progress in order to provide optimum safety and health protection for their workers;

Whereas the ergonomic aspects are of particular importance for a VDU workstation:

Article 1

This Directive, which is an individual Directive within the meaning of Article 16 of the Directive on the introduction of measures to encourage improvements in the safety and health of workers at work, lays down minimum requirements for safety and health for work with VDUs as defined in Article 2.

Article 2

For the purposes of this Directive, the following terms have the meaning hereby assigned to them:

- 'Visual display unit': an alphanumeric screen, regardless of the display process employed.
- 'Workstation': an assembly that may comprise the following: display screen, keyboard, peripherals, including diskette drive, printer, document holder, work chair, work desk and the immediate work environment.
- 'Worker': any worker who regularly uses a VDU, even if only for part of the time.

Article 3

1 The Member States shall provide for adequate checks and supervision to ensure the implementation of this Directive.

Article 4

1 Employers shall be obliged to perform an analysis of workstations in order to evaluate the safety and health conditions to which they give rise for their workers (particularly as regards possible risks to eyesight, physical problems and problems of mental stress).
2 They shall take appropriate measures to eliminate the risks found.

Article 5

Workstations put into service after the entry into force of this Directive shall take into account the minimum requirements laid down in the Annex to this Directive.

Article 6

Workstations already in place when this Directive enters into force shall be adapted to comply with the minimum requirements laid down in the Annex not later than two years after the entry into force of this Directive.

Article 6a

Workers or their representatives shall be entitled to submit proposals to the employer concerning specific measures regarding the organisation and equipping of VDU workstations.

Article 7

1 Every worker who uses a VDU at his/her workstation shall receive training in its use before commencing this type of work and whenever the organisation of the workstation is substantially modified.

2 Workers shall receive information on all aspects of health and safety relating to their workstation, including the possible effects on their eyes and physical or mental problems.

Article 7a

The employer shall ensure that daily working time on a VDU is appropriately divided up and to arrange for employees to take periodic breaks away from the screen or have a change in activity.

Article 8

Workers or their representatives:

– shall be consulted on the implementation of the provisions of Articles 5 and 6.

– shall take part in deciding the arrangements for dividing up daily working time on VDUs.

Article 9

Workers shall be entitled to have an appropriate ophthalmological examination prior to commencing VDU work and at regular intervals thereafter.

The worker shall be provided with special glasses tested for the work concerned if an ophthalmological examination shows that they are required and that glasses intended for normal purposes cannot be used.

These tests, and any subsequent ophthalmological examination, and any glasses specifically prescribed for use with VDUs may in no circumstances involve workers in additional financial cost.

Annex

1 Display Screen

The characters on the screen shall be well-defined and clearly formed, of adequate size and with adequate spacing between the characters and lines. The image of the screen should be stable, with no flickering or other forms of instability. The brightness contrast between the characters and the background shall be easily adjustable by the operator. The screen shall be easily and freely rotatable and tiltable to suit the needs of the operator. It shall be possible to use a separate base for the screen or an adjustable table. The screen shall be free of reflections.

2 Keyboard

The keyboard shall be inclined and separate from the screen so as to allow the worker to find a comfortable working position avoiding muscle fatigue in the arms or hands. The space in front of the keyboard shall be sufficient to provide support for the hands and arms of the operator.

The keyboard shall have a matt surface to avoid reflective glare; the keys shall have low-reflectance surfaces and concave tops.

The symbols on the keys shall be adequately contrasted.

3 Work Desk

The work desk shall have a sufficiently large, low-reflectance surface and allow a flexible arrangement of the screen, keyboard, documents and related equipment.

The document holder shall be situated on the desk on the same level as the display screen to minimize the need for rapid head and eye movements.

Adequate leg space is necessary.

4 Work Chair

The work chair shall be stable but allow the worker easy freedom of movement.

The seat shall be adjustable in height. The seat back shall be adjustable in both height and tilt to ensure a comfortable position for the operator. A footrest shall be made available to anyone who wishes one.

5 Lighting

Suitable ambient lighting is required so as to provide satisfactory working conditions and an appropriate contrast between the screen and the background environment.

Lamps for secondary activities shall be provided where necessary; they shall be adjustable but shall not cause glare or reflections on the screen.

6 Reflections and Glare

Workstations shall be designed so that sources of light cause no direct glare and, as far as possible, no reflections on the screen.

Windows shall be fitted with a suitable system of adjustable covering.

7 Noise

Noise from equipment (printer, diskette drive, built-in fan, etc.) shall be taken into account when the workstation is being equipped, in particular so as not to distract attention or disturb speech.

8 Heat

The heat generated by computer equipment shall not cause discomfort.

9 Radiation

A constant effort shall be made to reduce the radiation emitted by equipment that includes a display screen.

10 Humidity

An adequate level of humidity shall be established and maintained.

11   *Operator/Computer Interface*

The psycho-social factors applicable to the writing of programs (software) and to the tasks resulting from such programs shall be taken into account; no clandestine individual checks (tell-tale devices) may be built into the programs.

The principles of software ergonomics shall be applied in particular to human data processing.

Appendix III
Where to Go for Help and Further Reading

If you are in a union you should approach your shop steward or staff representative in the first instance. There is great value in the issues being discussed at a meeting of *all* the staff who may (or may not) be affected by the problem(s). Should this fail, or should you be the staff representative or shop steward, you may need to go to your union's full-time office for advice and/or the local branch/area meeting of your trade union.

Further help and advice is available, in some instances to non-union members, from the trade union resource or hazards centres listed below.

If you are not in a union then, as this book has argued throughout, you and your fellow workers should think of joining one and forming a workplace branch to help solve or mitigate your problems. Advice about joining a union is available from the trade union resource centres listed below, your local trades union council (in the telephone directory) or possibly at your local law centre, citizens' advice bureau or Labour Party office. The Trade Union Congress (Congress House, Great Russell Street, London WC1B 3LS) may also be of help.

Finally, if you approach them as an individual, the agencies mentioned – local trade union advice centres, hazards centres, occupational health projects, law centres, citizens' advice bureaux, etc. – may be able to help you with information and advice; although for reasons of time, many prefer to deal mainly with groups of people.

Work Hazard Groups, Local Trade Union Health and Safety Groups and Resource Centres

Birmingham Region Union Safety and Health Campaign (BRUSH)
Unit 304
The Argent Centre
60 Fredrick Street
Birmingham B1 3HS
Telephone 021–236 0801

Coventry Workshop
38 Binley Road
Coventry CV3 1JA
Telephone 0203 27772/3

Greater Manchester Hazards Centre
23 New Mount Street
Manchester M4 4DE
Telephone 061–953 4037

Health and Safety Advice Centre
Unit 304
The Argent Centre
60 Fredrick Street
Birmingham B1 3HS
Telephone 021–236 0801

Health and Safety Project
Trade Union Studies Information Unit
Southend Fernwood Road
Jesmond
Newcastle NE2 1TJ
Telephone 091–281 6087

Hull Action on Safety and Health
31 Ferens Avenue
Cottingham Road
Hull HU6 7SY
Telephone 0482 213496

Isle of Wight Trade Union Safety Group
Bob Davies
12 Winston Road
Newport
Isle of Wight PO30 1RF
Telephone IOW 520439

Liverpool TUC Health and Safety Committee and Trade Union Resource Centre
24 Hardman Street
Liverpool L1 9AX
Telephone 051–709 3995

London Hazards Centre
3rd Floor Headland House
308 Gray's Inn Road
London WC1X 8DS
Telephone 071–837 5605

Lothian Trade Union and Community Resource Centre
12a Picardy Place
Edinburgh EH1 3JT
Telephone 031–556 7318

Nottingham TUC Safety and Health Committee
c/o 118 Mansfield Road
Nottingham
Telephone 0602 281898

Portsmouth Area Health and Safety Group
Norman Harvey
32 Rowner Close
Gosport,
Hants PO13 0LY
Telephone 0329 281898

Sheffield Area Trade Union Safety Committee
3rd Floor
Town Hall Chambers
Barkers Pool
Sheffield S1 1EN
Telephone 0742 753834

Sheffield Occupational Health Project
Birley Moor Health Centre
2 Eastgate Crescent
Sheffield S12 4QN
Telephone 0742 645691

South East Scotland Hazards Group
10 Fountainhall Road
Edinburgh
Telephone 031–667 1081 ex. 2932

VDU Workers' Rights Campaign
c/o City Centre
32–35 Featherstone Street
London EC1
Telephone 071–608 1338

Walsall Action for Safety and Health
7 Edinburgh Drive
Rushall
Walsall WS4 1HW
Telephone 0922 25860

West Yorkshire Hazards Group
Box 22
Bradford Resource Centre
31 Manor Row
Bradford BD1 4PS
Telephone 0274 725046

Women and Work Hazards Group
London Women's Centre
Wesley House
4 Wild Court
London WC2B 5AX

Further Sources of Information and Help

City Centre
32–35 Featherstone Street
London EC1
Telephone 071–608 1338
City Centre is an advice and information centre for office workers in London.

Childcare Now
Wesley House
4 Wild Court
London WC2B 5AX
Telephone 071–831 6946

Immunity
260a Kilburn Lane
London W10 4BE
Legal advice on AIDS/HIV

LAGER (Lesbian and Gay Employment Rights)
St Margaret's House
21 Old Ford Road
London E2 9PL
Telephone 081–983 0696

Lesbian Employment Rights
St Margaret's House
21 Old Ford Road
London E2 9PL
Telephone 081–983 0694

Women Against Sexual Harassment
242 Pentonville Road
London N1 9UN
Telephone 071–833 0222

Women's Design Service
18 Ashwin Street
London E8 3DL
Telephone 071–241 6910
Women's Design Service provides information and resources on
women and the built environment

Workplace Nurseries Campaign
77 Holloway Road
London N7 8JZ
Telephone 071–700 0281

Information About Trade Unions

Trades Union Congress
Congress House
Great Russell Street
London WC1B 3LS
Telephone 071–636 4030

J. Eaton and C. Gill, *The Trade Union Directory – A Guide to all TUC Unions*, Pluto Press (1981).

White-collar Trade Unions Representing Office Workers

(Contacts for lesbian and gay, black, disabled, and women trade union members' committees, groups or sections are listed under each trade union, where relevant. If no contact is given, office workers should refer to their own unions for information.)

Association of Cinematograph, Television and Allied Technicians (ACTT)

111 Wardour Street
London W1V 4AY
Telephone 071–437 8506

Sexuality Committee,
Disability Committee and
Women Members' Committee
c/o The Equality Office
address and telephone as above

Banking, Insurance and Finance Union (BIFU)

Sheffield House
1b Amity Grove
Raynes Park
London SW20 0LG
Telephone 081–946 9151

Lesbian and gay members'
contact: Peter Freeman
25 Ferrara Square
Swansea SA1 1UW

Civil and Public Services Association (CPSA)
160 Falcon Road
London SE11 2LN
Telephone 071–924 2727

Lesbian and gay members'
contact: c/o 74 Cecil Road
London E17 5DJ
Telephone 081–520 0935 x262 (w)

GMB (Britain's General Union)
Thorne House
Ruxley Ridge
Claygate
Esher
Surrey KT10 0TL
Telephone 0372 62081

Inland Revenue Staff Federation
Douglas Houghton House
231 Vauxhall Bridge Road
London SW1V 1EH
Telephone 071–834 8254

Manufacturing, Science and Finance (MSF)
79 Camden Road
London NW1 9ES
Telephone 071–267 4422

Lesbian and gay members'
contact: address as above
National Advisory Committee for Disability and Employment
c/o MSF
address and telephone as above

National and Local Government Officers' Association (NALGO)
1 Mabledon Place
London WC1H 9AJ
Telephone 071–388 2366

Lesbian and gay members' contacts:

Eastern District – Phillip
Telephone 0603–223 281 (daytime)

Glasgow & West – Linda McLaughlin
53 Cochrane St
Glasgow G2

Islington Workers Group – Peter Watkins
2 Orleston Road
London N7 8LH
Telephone 071–354 7470

London Metropolitan District – NALGO Office
Civic Centre
High Street
Uxbridge
Middlesex

South East District – Linda Webster
District Office
179 Preston Road
Brighton
Telephone 0273–542 244

National Lesbian and Gay Steering Committee,
National Disability Committee, and
National Women's Committee
c/o NALGO Head Office
address as before

National Black Members' Co-ordinating Committee
c/o Camden Black Workers' Group
Camden Town Hall
Judd Street
London NW1 2RU

National Communication Union (NCU)
Greystoke House
150 Brunswick Road
London W5 1AW
Telephone 081–998 2981

National Union of Civil and Public Servants (NUCPS)
124–130 Southwark Street
London SE1 0TU
Telephone 071–928 9671

Lesbian and gay members'
contact: Cathy
Telephone 071–865 4510 (w)

National Union of Journalists (NUJ)
Acorn House
314 Gray's Inn Road
London WC1X 8DP
Telephone 071–278 7916

Disabled members' contact:
c/o The Equality Committee
address and telephone as above

Society of Graphical and Allied Trades '82 (SOGAT '82)
Sogat House, 274–288 London Road
Hadleigh
Benfleet
Essex SS7 2DE
Telephone 0702 554111

Union of Communication Workers (UCW)
UCW House
Crescent Lane
Clapham
London SW4 9RN
Telephone 071–622 2442

Videos and Further Reading

Asbestos

Institution of Environmental Health Officers, *Asbestos in Buildings*, VHS Video, IEHO, 1986.

Labour Research Department, *Fighting asbestos at work and at home*, LRD Publications, 1985.

People's Asbestos Action Campaign, *Asbestos Fact Pack*, PAAC, c/o London Hazards Centre, 1987.

Ergonomics

E. Grandjean, *Fitting the task to the man* (sic), Taylor and Francis, 1988.

General and Office Hazards

London Hazards Centre, *Daily Hazard*, Newsletter of the London Hazards Centre (five issues per year).

Hazards Publications Ltd, *Hazards Bulletin*, a magazine for safety representatives (five issues per year).

City Centre, *Safer Office Bulletin*, City Centre (four issues per year).

Health and Safety Law

Trades Union Congress, *TUC guide to health and safety*, TUC Publications, 1985.

Lesbian and Gay Rights at Work

Trades Unionists Against Section 28, *Out at work: campaigning for lesbian and gay rights*, published in association with *City Limits*, 1989.

Lighting

Health and Safety Executive, *Lighting at Work*, HMSO, 1987.

London Hazards Centre, *Fluorescent Lighting – A health hazard overhead*, London Hazards Centre Trust, 1987.

New Technology and VDUs

U. Huws, *VDU Hazards Handbook – A worker's guide to new technology*, London Hazards Centre Trust, 1987.

Labour Research Department, *VDUs, Health and Jobs*, LRD Publications, 1985.

Team Video, *Technology at Work*, Team Video Productions, (undated).

Noise

Trades Union Congress, *TUC Handbook on Noise at Work*, TUC Publications, 1986.

Repetition Strain Injuries

Margot Nash, *Teno – a film about tenosynovitis*, Cinema of Women, 1984.

Team Video, *Repetitive Strain Injuries at Work*, Team Video Productions (undated).

London Hazards Centre, *Repetition Strain Injuries – Hidden harm from overuse*, London Hazards Centre Trust, 1988.

Sexual Harassment at Work, Ann Sedley and Melissa Benn, NCCL, 1982.

Sick Building Syndrome

London Hazards Centre, *Sick Building Syndrome*, London Hazards Centre Trust, 1990.

TV Choice, *Sick Buildings – the battle for healthier offices*, TV Choice, 1989.

Stress

Labour Research Department, *Stress at Work*, LRD Publications, 1988.

Labour Research Department, *Workplace Health – a trade union guide*, LRD Publications, 1989.

Trade Union and Bargaining Information

Labour Research Department, *Labour Research* and *Bargaining Report*, LRD Publications, monthly magazines.

Women and Work Hazards

Audrey Droisen and Women and Work Hazards Group, *Bitter Wages*, Video, Cinema of Women, 1984.

W. Chavkin, *Double Exposure – Women's health hazards on the job and at home*, New Feminist Library, New York, 1984.

Index